Shakespeare
Explained

The
Tempest

SUSAN H. KRUEGER
INTRODUCTION BY JOSEPH SOBRAN

Marshall Cavendish
Benchmark
New York

Series consultant: Richard Larkin

Marshall Cavendish
99 White Plains Road
Tarrytown, New York 10591
www.marshallcavendish.us

Library of Congress Cataloging-in-Publication Data
Krueger, Susan Heidi.
The tempest / by Susan Heidi Krueger.
p. cm. — (Shakespeare explained)
Includes bibliographical references and index.
Summary: "A literary analysis of the play The Tempest. Includes information on
the history and culture of Elizabethan England"—Provided by publisher.
ISBN 978-0-7614-3423-8
1. Shakespeare, William, 1564-1616. Tempest—Juvenile literature. I. Title.
PR2833.K77 2009
822.3'3—dc22
2009002587

Photo research by: Linda Sykes
istockphoto: cover; Ian Jeffrey/istockphoto: 2-3; Raciro/istockphoto: 4; Art Parts RF: 6, 8, 13, 24, 25;
©Nik Wheeler/Corbis: 11; Portraitgalerie, Schloss Ambras, Innsbruck, Austria/Erich Lessing/Art
Resource, NY: 18; AA World Travel Library/Alamy: 20; ©Hideo Kurihara/Alamy: 22; Corbis/Sygma:
27; Andrew Fox/Corbis: 30; The Everett Collection: 37, 45, 87; Christie's Images/Corbis: 41;
T. Charles Erickson: 48; Hugo Glendinning/Royal Shakespeare Company: 50, 63; Henrietta Butler/
ArenaPAL/Topfoto/The Image Works: 55; Manuel Harlan/Royal Shakespeare Company: 61;
Clive Barda/Arenapal/Topfoto/The Image Works: 66; Tristram Kenton/Lebrecht Music & Arts: 70;
The Bridgeman Art Library: 74; NBC/The Everett Collection: 81; Robbie Jack/Corbis: 83.

Editor: Deborah Grahame
Publisher: Michelle Bisson
Art Director: Anahid Hamparian
Series Design: Kay Petronio

Printed in Malaysia
135642

Contents

66929

Shakespeare and His World

WILLIAM SHAKESPEARE, OFTEN NICKNAMED "THE BARD," IS, BEYOND ANY COMPARISON, THE MOST TOWERING NAME IN ENGLISH LITERATURE. MANY CONSIDER HIS PLAYS THE GREATEST EVER WRITTEN. HE STANDS OUT EVEN AMONG GENIUSES.

Yet the Bard is also closer to our hearts than lesser writers, and his tremendous reputation should neither intimidate us nor prevent us from enjoying the simple delights he offers in such abundance. It is as if he had written for each of us personally. As he himself put it, "One touch of nature makes the whole world kin."

Such tragedies as *Hamlet*, *Romeo and Juliet*, and *Macbeth* are world famous, still performed onstage and in films. These and other plays have also been adapted for radio, television, opera, ballet, pantomime, novels, comic books, and other media. Two of the best ways to become familiar with them are to watch some of the many fine movies that have been made of them and to listen to recordings of them by some of the world's great actors.

Even Shakespeare's individual characters have lives of their own, like real historical figures. Hamlet is still regarded as the most challenging role ever written for an actor. Roughly as many whole books have been written about Hamlet, an imaginary character, as about actual historical figures such as Abraham Lincoln and Napoleon Bonaparte.

Shakespeare created an amazing variety of vivid characters. One of Shakespeare's most peculiar traits was that he loved his characters so much—even some of his villains and secondary or comic characters—that at times he let them run away with the play, stealing attention from his heroes and heroines.

So in *A Midsummer Night's Dream* audiences remember the absurd and lovable fool Bottom the Weaver better than the lovers who are the main characters. Romeo's friend Mercutio is more fiery and witty than Romeo himself; legend claims that Shakespeare said he had to kill Mercutio or Mercutio would have killed the play.

Shakespeare also wrote dozens of comedies and historical plays, as well as nondramatic poems. Although his tragedies are now regarded as his greatest works, he freely mixed them with comedy and history. And his sonnets are among the supreme love poems in the English language.

It is Shakespeare's mastery of the English language that keeps his words familiar to us today. Every literate person knows dramatic lines such as "Wherefore art thou Romeo?"; "My kingdom for a horse!"; "To be or not to be: that is the question"; "Friends, Romans, countrymen, lend me your ears"; and "What fools these mortals be!" Shakespeare's sonnets are noted for their sweetness: "Shall I compare thee to a summer's day?"

WHAT'S PAST IS PROLOGUE.

SHAKESPEARE'S LANGUAGE

WITHOUT A DOUBT, SHAKESPEARE WAS THE GREATEST MASTER OF THE ENGLISH LANGUAGE WHO EVER LIVED. BUT JUST WHAT DOES THAT MEAN?

Shakespeare's vocabulary was huge, full of references to the Bible as well as Greek and Roman mythology. Yet his most brilliant phrases often combine very simple and familiar words:

"WHAT'S IN A NAME? THAT WHICH WE CALL A ROSE BY ANY OTHER NAME WOULD SMELL AS SWEET."

He has delighted countless millions of readers. And we know him only through his language. He has shaped modern English far more than any other writer.

Or, to put it in more personal terms, you probably quote his words several times every day without realizing it, even if you have never suspected that Shakespeare could be a source of pleasure to you.

So why do so many English-speaking readers find his language so difficult? It is our language, too, but it has changed so much that it is no longer quite the same language—nor a completely different one, either.

Shakespeare's English and ours overlap without being identical. He would have some difficulty understanding us, too! Many of our everyday words and phrases would baffle him.

Shakespeare, for example, would not know what we meant by a *car*, a *radio*, a *movie*, a *television*, a *computer*, or a *sitcom*, since these things did not even exist in his time. Our old-fashioned term *railroad train* would be unimaginable to him, far in the distant future. We would have to explain to him (if we could) what *nuclear weapons*, *electricity*, and *democracy* are. He would also be a little puzzled by common expressions such as *high-tech, feel the heat, approval ratings, war criminal, judgmental,* and *whoopie cushion*.

So how can we call him "the greatest master of the English language"? It might seem as if he barely spoke English at all! (He would, however, recognize much of our dirty slang, even if he pronounced it slightly differently. His plays also contain many racial insults to Jews, Africans, Italians, Irish, and others. Today he would be called "insensitive.")

Many of the words of Shakespeare's time have become archaic. Words like *thou, thee, thy, thyself,* and *thine,* which were among the most common words in the language in Shakespeare's day, have all but disappeared today. We simply say *you* for both singular and plural, formal and familiar. Most other modern languages have kept their *thou*.

Sometimes the same words now have different meanings. We are apt to be misled by such simple, familiar words as *kind, wonderful, waste, just,* and *dear,* which he often uses in ways that differ from our usage.

Shakespeare also doesn't always use the words we expect to hear, the words that we ourselves would naturally use. When we might automatically say, "I beg your pardon" or just "Sorry," he might say, "I cry you mercy."

Often a glossary and footnotes will solve all three of these problems for us. But it is most important to bear in mind that Shakespeare was often hard for his first audiences to understand. Even in his own time his rich language was challenging. And this was deliberate. Shakespeare was inventing his own kind of English. It remains unique today.

A child doesn't learn to talk by using a dictionary. Children learn first by sheer immersion. We teach babies by pointing at things and saying their names. Yet the toddler always learns faster than we can teach! Even as babies we are geniuses. Dictionaries can help us later, when we already speak and read the language well (and learn more slowly).

So the best way to learn Shakespeare is not to depend on the footnotes and glossary too much, but instead to be like a baby: just get into the flow of the language. Go to performances of the plays or watch movies of them.

THE LANGUAGE HAS A MAGICAL WAY OF TEACHING ITSELF, IF WE LET IT. THERE IS NO REASON TO FEEL STUPID OR FRUSTRATED WHEN IT DOESN'T COME EASILY.

Hundreds of phrases have entered the English language from *Hamlet* alone, including "to hold, as t'were, the mirror up to nature"; "murder most foul"; "the thousand natural shocks that flesh is heir to"; "flaming youth"; "a countenance more in sorrow than in anger"; "the play's the thing"; "neither a borrower nor a lender be"; "in my mind's eye"; "something is rotten in the state of Denmark"; "alas, poor Yorick"; and "the lady doth protest too much, methinks."

From other plays we get the phrases "star-crossed lovers"; "what's in a name?"; "we have scotched the snake, not killed it"; "one fell swoop"; "it was Greek to me"; "I come to bury Caesar, not to praise him"; and "the most unkindest cut of all"—all these are among our household words. In fact, Shakespeare even gave us the expression "household words." No wonder his contemporaries marveled at his "fine filed phrase" and swooned at the "mellifluous and honey-tongued Shakespeare."

Shakespeare's words seem to combine music, magic, wisdom, and humor:

"THE COURSE OF TRUE LOVE NEVER DID RUN SMOOTH."

"HE JESTS AT SCARS THAT NEVER FELT A WOUND."

"THE FAULT, DEAR BRUTUS, IS NOT IN OUR STARS, BUT IN OURSELVES, THAT WE ARE UNDERLINGS."

"COWARDS DIE MANY TIMES BEFORE THEIR DEATHS; THE VALIANT NEVER TASTE OF DEATH BUT ONCE."

"NOT THAT I LOVED CAESAR LESS, BUT THAT I LOVED ROME MORE."

"THERE ARE MORE THINGS IN HEAVEN AND EARTH, HORATIO, THAN ARE DREAMT OF IN YOUR PHILOSOPHY."

"BREVITY IS THE SOUL OF WIT."

"THERE'S A DIVINITY THAT SHAPES OUR ENDS, ROUGH-HEW THEM HOW WE WILL."

Four centuries after Shakespeare lived, to speak English is to quote him. His huge vocabulary and linguistic fertility are still astonishing. He has had a powerful effect on all of us, whether we realize it or not. We may wonder how it is even possible for a single human being to say so many memorable things.

Only the King James translation of the Bible, perhaps, has had a more profound and pervasive influence on the English language than Shakespeare. And, of course, the Bible was written by many authors over many centuries, and the King James translation, published in 1611, was the combined effort of many scholars.

EARLY LIFE

So who, exactly, was Shakespeare? Mystery surrounds his life, largely because few records were kept during his time. Some people have even doubted his identity, arguing that the real author of Shakespeare's plays must have been a man of superior formal education and wide experience. In a sense such doubts are a natural and understandable reaction to his rare, almost miraculous powers of expression, but some people feel that the doubts themselves show a lack of respect for the supremely human poet.

Most scholars agree that Shakespeare was born in the town of Stratford-upon-Avon in the county of Warwickshire, England, in April 1564. He was baptized, according to local church records, Gulielmus (William) Shakspere (the name was spelled in several different ways) on April 26 of that year. He was one of several children, most of whom died young.

His father, John Shakespeare (or Shakspere), was a glove maker and, at times, a town official. He was often in debt or being fined for unknown delinquencies, perhaps failure to attend church regularly. It is suspected that John was a recusant (secret and illegal) Catholic, but there is no proof. Many

SHAKESPEARE'S CHILDHOOD HOME IS CARED FOR BY AN INDEPENDENT CHARITY, THE SHAKESPEARE BIRTHPLACE TRUST, IN STRATFORD-UPON-AVON, WARWICKSHIRE, ENGLAND.

scholars have found Catholic tendencies in Shakespeare's plays, but whether Shakespeare was Catholic or not we can only guess.

At the time of Shakespeare's birth, England was torn by religious controversy and persecution. The country had left the Roman Catholic Church during the reign of King Henry VIII, who had died in 1547. Two of Henry's children, Edward and Mary, ruled after his death. When his daughter Elizabeth I became queen in 1558, she upheld his claim that the monarch of England was also head of the English Church.

Did William attend the local grammar school? He was probably entitled to, given his father's prominence in Stratford, but again, we face a frustrating absence of proof, and many people of the time learned to read very well without schooling. If he went to the town school, he would also have learned the rudiments of Latin.

We know very little about the first half of William's life. In 1582, when he was eighteen, he married Anne Hathaway, eight years his senior. Their first daughter, Susanna, was born six months later. The following year they had twins, Hamnet and Judith.

At this point William disappears from the records again. By the early 1590s we find "William Shakespeare" in London, a member of the city's leading acting company, called the Lord Chamberlain's Men. Many of Shakespeare's greatest roles, we are told, were first performed by the company's star, Richard Burbage.

Curiously, the first work published under (and identified with) Shakespeare's name was not a play but a long erotic poem, *Venus and Adonis*, in 1593. It was dedicated to the young Earl of Southampton, Henry Wriothesley.

Venus and Adonis was a spectacular success, and Shakespeare was immediately hailed as a major poet. In 1594 he dedicated a longer, more serious poem to Southampton, *The Rape of Lucrece*. It was another hit, and for many years, these two poems were considered Shakespeare's greatest works, despite the popularity of his plays.

"YOUR TALE, SIR, WOULD CURE DEAFNESS."

TODAY MOVIES, NOT LIVE PLAYS, ARE THE MORE POPULAR ART FORM. FORTUNATELY MOST OF SHAKESPEARE'S PLAYS HAVE BEEN FILMED, AND THE BEST OF THESE MOVIES OFFER AN EXCELLENT WAY TO MAKE THE BARD'S ACQUAINTANCE. RECENTLY, KENNETH BRANAGH HAS BECOME A RESPECTED CONVERTER OF SHAKESPEARE'S PLAYS INTO FILM.

Hamlet

Hamlet, Shakespeare's most famous play, has been well filmed several times. In 1948 Laurence Olivier won three Academy Awards—for best picture, best actor, and best director—for his version of the play. The film allowed him to show some of the magnetism that made him famous on the stage. Nobody spoke Shakespeare's lines more thrillingly.

The young Derek Jacobi played Hamlet in a 1980 BBC production of the play, with Patrick Stewart (now best known for *Star Trek, the Next Generation*) as the guilty king. Jacobi, like Olivier, has a gift for speaking the lines freshly; he never seems to be merely reciting the famous and familiar words. But whereas Olivier has animal passion, Jacobi is more intellectual. It is fascinating to compare the ways these two outstanding actors play Shakespeare's most complex character.

Franco Zeffirelli's 1990 *Hamlet*, starring Mel Gibson, is fascinating in a different way. Gibson, of course, is best known as an action hero, and he is not well suited to this supremely witty and introspective role, but Zeffirelli cuts the text drastically, and the result turns *Hamlet* into something that few people would have expected: a short, swiftly moving action movie. Several of the other characters are brilliantly played.

Henry IV, Part One

The 1979 BBC Shakespeare series production does a commendable job in this straightforward approach to the play. Battle scenes are effective despite obvious restrictions in an indoor studio setting. Anthony Quayle gives jovial Falstaff a darker edge, and Tim Pigott-Smith's Hotspur is buoyed by some humor. Jon Finch plays King Henry IV with noble authority, and David Gwillim gives Hal a surprisingly successful transformation from boy prince to heir apparent.

Julius Caesar

No really good movie of *Julius Caesar* exists, but the 1953 film, with Marlon Brando as Mark Antony, will do. James Mason is a thoughtful Brutus, and John Gielgud, then ranked with Laurence Olivier among the greatest Shakespearean actors, plays the villainous Cassius. The film is rather dull, and Brando is out of place in a Roman toga, but it is still worth viewing.

Macbeth

Roman Polanski is best known as a director of thrillers and horror films, so it may seem natural that he should have done his 1971 *The Tragedy of Macbeth* as an often-gruesome slasher flick. But this is also one of the most vigorous of all Shakespeare films. Macbeth and his wife are played by Jon Finch and Francesca Annis, neither known for playing Shakespeare, but they are young and attractive in roles that are usually given to older actors, which gives the story a fresh flavor.

The Merchant of Venice

Once again the matchless Sir Laurence Olivier delivers a great performance as Shylock with his wife Joan Plowright as Portia in the 1974 TV film, adapted from the 1970 National Theater (of Britain) production. A 1980 BBC offering features Warren Mitchell as Shylock and Gemma Jones as Portia, with John Rhys-Davies as Salerio. The most recent production, starring Al Pacino as Shylock, Jeremy Irons as Antonio, and Joseph Fiennes as Bassanio, was filmed in Venice and released in 2004.

A Midsummer Night's Dream

Because of the prestige of his tragedies, we tend to forget how many comedies Shakespeare wrote—nearly twice the number of tragedies. Of these perhaps the most popular has always been the enchanting, atmospheric, and very silly masterpiece *A Midsummer Night's Dream*.

In more recent times several films have been made of *A Midsummer Night's Dream*. Among the more notable have been Max Reinhardt's 1935 black-and-white version, with Mickey Rooney (then a child star) as Puck.

Of the several film versions, the one starring Kevin Kline as Bottom and Stanley Tucci as Puck, made in 1999 with nineteenth-century costumes and directed by Michael Hoffman, ranks among the finest, and is surely one of the most sumptuous to watch.

Othello

Orson Welles did a budget European version in 1952, now available as a restored DVD. Laurence Olivier's 1965 film performance is predictably remarkable, though it has been said that he would only approach the part by honoring, even emulating, Paul Robeson's definitive interpretation that ran on Broadway in 1943. (Robeson was the first black actor to play Othello, the Moor of Venice, and he did so to critical acclaim, though sadly his performance was never filmed.) Maggie Smith plays a formidable Desdemona opposite Olivier, and her youth and energy will surprise younger audiences who know her only from the Harry Potter films. Laurence Fishburne brilliantly portrayed Othello in the 1995 film, costarring with Kenneth Branagh as a surprisingly human Iago, though Irène Jacob's Desdemona was disappointingly weak.

Romeo and Juliet

This, the world's most famous love story, has been filmed many times, twice very successfully over the last generation. Franco Zeffirelli directed a hit version in 1968 with Leonard Whiting and the rapturously pretty Olivia Hussey, set in Renaissance Italy. Baz Luhrmann made a much more contemporary version, with a loud rock score, starring Leonardo DiCaprio and Claire Danes, in 1996.

It seems safe to say that Shakespeare would have preferred Zeffirelli's movie, with its superior acting and rich, romantic, sun-drenched Italian scenery.

The Tempest

A 1960 Hallmark Hall of Fame production featured Maurice Evans as Prospero, Lee Remick as Miranda, Roddy McDowall as Ariel, and Richard Burton as Caliban. The special effects are primitive and the costumes are ludicrous, but it moves along at a fast pace. Another TV version aired in 1998 and was nominated for a Golden Globe. Peter Fonda played Gideon Prosper, and Katherine Heigl played his daughter Miranda Prosper. Sci-fi fans may already know that the classic 1956 film *Forbidden Planet* is modeled on themes and characters from the play.

Twelfth Night

Trevor Nunn adapted the play for the 1996 film he also directed in a rapturous Edwardian setting, with big names like Helena Bonham Carter, Richard E. Grant, Imogen Stubbs, and Ben Kingsley as Feste. A 2003 film set in modern Britain provides an interesting multicultural experience; it features an Anglo-Indian cast with Parminder Nagra (*Bend It Like Beckham*) playing Viola. For the truly intrepid, a twelve-minute silent film made in 1910 does a fine job of capturing the play through visual gags and over-the-top gesturing.

THESE FILMS HAVE BEEN SELECTED FOR SEVERAL QUALITIES: APPEAL AND ACCESSIBILITY TO MODERN AUDIENCES, EXCELLENCE IN ACTING, PACING, VISUAL BEAUTY, AND, OF COURSE, FIDELITY TO SHAKESPEARE. THEY ARE THE MOTION PICTURES WE JUDGE MOST LIKELY TO HELP STUDENTS UNDERSTAND THE SOURCE OF THE BARD'S LASTING POWER.

SHAKESPEARE'S THEATER

Today we sometimes speak of "live entertainment." In Shakespeare's day, of course, all entertainment was live, because recordings, films, television, and radio did not yet exist. Even printed books were a novelty.

In fact, most communication in those days was difficult. Transportation was not only difficult but slow, chiefly by horse and boat. Most people were illiterate peasants who lived on farms that they seldom left; cities grew up along waterways and were subject to frequent plagues that could wipe out much of the population within weeks.

Money—in coin form, not paper—was scarce and hardly existed outside the cities. By today's standards, even the rich were poor. Life was precarious. Most children died young, and famine or disease might kill anyone at any time. Everyone was familiar with death. Starvation was not rare or remote, as it is to most of us today. Medical care was poor and might kill as many people as it healed.

This was the grim background of Shakespeare's theater during the reign of Queen Elizabeth I, who ruled from 1558 until her death in 1603. During that period England was also torn by religious conflict, often violent, among Roman

ELIZABETH I, A GREAT PATRON OF POETRY AND THE THEATER, WROTE SONNETS AND TRANSLATED CLASSIC WORKS.

Catholics who were loyal to the pope, adherents of the Church of England who were loyal to the queen, and the Puritans who would take over the country in the revolution of 1642.

Under these conditions, most forms of entertainment were luxuries that were out of most people's reach. The only way to hear music was to be in the actual physical presence of singers or musicians with their instruments, which were primitive by our standards.

One brutal form of entertainment, popular in London, was bearbaiting. A bear was blinded and chained to a stake, where fierce dogs called mastiffs were turned loose to tear him apart. The theaters had to compete with the bear gardens, as they were called, for spectators.

The Puritans, or radical Protestants, objected to bearbaiting and tried to ban it. Despite their modern reputation, the Puritans were anything but conservative. Conservative people, attached to old customs, hated the Puritans. They seemed to upset everything. (Many of America's first settlers, such as the Pilgrims who came over on the *Mayflower*, were dissidents who were fleeing the Church of England.)

Plays were extremely popular, but they were primitive, too. They had to be performed outdoors in the afternoon because of the lack of indoor lighting. Often the "theater" was only an enclosed courtyard. Probably the versions of Shakespeare's plays that we know today were not used in full, but shortened to about two hours for actual performance.

But eventually more regular theaters were built, featuring a raised stage extending into the audience. Poorer spectators (illiterate "groundlings") stood on the ground around it, at times exposed to rain and snow. Wealthier people sat in raised tiers above. Aside from some costumes, there were few props or special effects and almost no scenery. Much had to be imagined: Whole battles might be represented by a few actors with swords. Thunder might be simulated by rattling a sheet of tin offstage.

The plays were far from realistic and, under the conditions of the time, could hardly try to be. Above the rear of the main stage was a small balcony. (It was this balcony from which Juliet spoke to Romeo.) Ghosts and witches might appear by entering through a trapdoor in the stage floor.

Unlike the modern theater, Shakespeare's Globe Theater—he describes it as "this wooden O"—had no curtain separating the stage from the audience. This allowed intimacy between the players and the spectators.

THE RECONSTRUCTED GLOBE THEATER WAS COMPLETED IN 1997 AND IS LOCATED IN LONDON, JUST 200 YARDS (183 METERS) FROM THE SITE OF THE ORIGINAL.

"MY LIBRARY WAS DUKEDOM LARGE ENOUGH."

The spectators probably reacted rowdily to the play, not listening in reverent silence. After all, they had come to have fun! And few of them were scholars. Again, a play had to amuse people who could not read.

The lines of plays were written and spoken in prose or, more often, in a form of verse called iambic pentameter (ten syllables with five stresses per line). There was no attempt at modern realism. Only males were allowed on the stage, so some of the greatest women's roles ever written had to be played by boys or men. (The same is true, by the way, of the ancient Greek theater.)

Actors had to be versatile, skilled not only in acting, but also in fencing, singing, dancing, and acrobatics. Within its limitations, the theater offered a considerable variety of spectacles.

Plays were big business, not yet regarded as high art, sponsored by important and powerful people (the queen loved them as much as the groundlings did). The London acting companies also toured and performed in the provinces. When plagues struck London, the government might order the theaters to be closed to prevent the spread of disease among crowds. (They remained empty for nearly two years from 1593 to 1594.)

As the theater became more popular, the Puritans grew as hostile to it as they were to bearbaiting. Plays, like books, were censored by the government, and the Puritans fought to increase restrictions, eventually banning any mention of God and other sacred topics on the stage.

In 1642 the Puritans shut down all the theaters in London, and in 1644 they had the Globe demolished. The theaters remained closed until Charles's son, King Charles II, was restored to the throne in 1660 and the hated Puritans were finally vanquished.

But, by then, the tradition of Shakespeare's theater had been fatally interrupted. His plays remained popular, but they were often rewritten by inferior dramatists, and it was many years before they were performed (again) as he had originally written them.

THE ROYAL SHAKESPEARE THEATER, IN STRATFORD-UPON-AVON, WAS CLOSED IN 2007. A NEWLY DESIGNED INTERIOR WITH A 1,000-SEAT AUDITORIUM WILL BE COMPLETED IN 2010.

Today, of course, the plays are performed both in theaters and in films, sometimes in costumes of the period (ancient Rome for *Julius Caesar*, medieval England for *Henry V*), sometimes in modern dress (*Richard III* has recently been reset in England in the 1930s).

PLAYS

In the England of Queen Elizabeth I, plays were enjoyed by all classes of people, but they were not yet respected as a serious form of art.

Shakespeare's plays began to appear in print in individual, or quarto, editions in 1594, but none of these bore his name until 1598. Although his tragedies are now ranked as his supreme achievements, his name was first associated with comedies and with plays about English history.

The dates of Shakespeare's plays are notoriously hard to determine. Few performances of them were documented; some were not printed until decades after they first appeared on the stage. Mainstream scholars generally place most of the comedies and histories in the 1590s, admitting that this time frame is no more than a widely accepted estimate.

The three parts of *King Henry VI*, culminating in a fourth part, *Richard III*, deal with the long and complex dynastic struggle or civil wars known as the Wars of the Roses (1455–1487), one of England's most turbulent periods. Today it is not easy to follow the plots of these plays.

It may seem strange to us that a young playwright should have written such demanding works early in his career, but they were evidently very popular with the Elizabethan public. Of the four, only *Richard III*, with its wonderfully villainous starring role, is still often performed.

Even today, one of Shakespeare's early comedies, *The Taming of the Shrew*, remains a crowd-pleaser. (It has enjoyed success in a 1999 film adaptation, *10 Things I Hate About You*, with Heath Ledger and Julia Stiles.) The story is simple: The enterprising Petruchio resolves to marry a rich

THE "REAL" SHAKESPEARE

AROUND 1850 DOUBTS STARTED TO SURFACE ABOUT WHO HAD ACTUALLY WRITTEN SHAKESPEARE'S PLAYS, CHIEFLY BECAUSE MANY OTHER AUTHORS, SUCH AS MARK TWAIN, THOUGHT THE PLAYS' AUTHOR WAS TOO WELL EDUCATED AND KNOWLEDGEABLE TO HAVE BEEN THE MODESTLY SCHOOLED MAN FROM STRATFORD.

Who, then, was the real author? Many answers have been given, but the three leading candidates are Francis Bacon, Christopher Marlowe, and Edward de Vere, Earl of Oxford.

Francis Bacon (1561-1626)

Bacon was a distinguished lawyer, scientist, philosopher, and essayist. Many considered him one of the great geniuses of his time, capable of any literary achievement, though he wrote little poetry and, as far as we know, no dramas. When people began to suspect that "Shakespeare" was only a pen name, he seemed like a natural candidate. But his writing style was vastly different from the style of the plays.

Christopher Marlowe (1564–1593)

Marlowe wrote several excellent tragedies in a style much like that of the Shakespeare tragedies, though without the comic blend. But he was reportedly killed in a mysterious incident in 1593, before most of the Bard's plays existed. Could his death have been faked? Is it possible that he lived on for decades in hiding, writing under a pen name? This is what his advocates contend.

Edward de Vere, Earl of Oxford (1550–1604)

Oxford is now the most popular and plausible alternative to the lad from Stratford. He had a high reputation as a poet and playwright in his day, but his life was full of scandal. That controversial life seems to match what the poet says about himself in the sonnets, as well as many events in the plays (especially *Hamlet*). However, he died in 1604, and most scholars believe this rules him out as the author of plays that were published after that date.

THE GREAT MAJORITY OF EXPERTS REJECT THESE AND ALL OTHER ALTERNATIVE CANDIDATES, STICKING WITH THE TRADITIONAL VIEW, AFFIRMED IN THE 1623 FIRST FOLIO OF THE PLAYS, THAT THE AUTHOR WAS THE MAN FROM STRATFORD. THAT REMAINS THE SAFEST POSITION TO TAKE, UNLESS STARTLING NEW EVIDENCE TURNS UP, WHICH, AT THIS LATE DATE, SEEMS HIGHLY UNLIKELY.

young woman, Katherina Minola, for her wealth, despite her reputation for having a bad temper. Nothing she does can discourage this dauntless suitor, and the play ends with Kate becoming a submissive wife. It is all the funnier for being unbelievable.

With *Romeo and Juliet* the Bard created his first enduring triumph. This tragedy of "star-crossed lovers" from feuding families is known around the world. Even people with only the vaguest knowledge of Shakespeare are often aware of this universally beloved story. It has inspired countless similar stories and adaptations, such as the hit musical *West Side Story*.

By the mid-1590s Shakespeare was successful and prosperous, a partner in the Lord Chamberlain's Men. He was rich enough to buy New Place, one of the largest houses in his hometown of Stratford.

Yet, at the peak of his good fortune came the worst sorrow of his life: Hamnet, his only son, died in August 1596 at the age of eleven, leaving nobody to carry on his family name, which was to die out with his two daughters.

Our only evidence of his son's death is a single line in the parish burial register. As far as we know, this crushing loss left no mark on Shakespeare's work. As far as his creative life shows, it was as if nothing had happened. His silence about his grief may be the greatest puzzle of his mysterious life, although, as we shall see, others remain.

During this period, according to traditional dating (even if it must be somewhat hypothetical), came the torrent of Shakespeare's mightiest works. Among these was another quartet of English history plays, this one centering on the legendary King Henry IV, including *Richard II* and the two parts of *Henry IV*.

Then came a series of wonderful romantic comedies: *Much Ado About Nothing*, *As You Like It*, and *Twelfth Night*.

In 1598 the clergyman Francis Meres, as part of a larger work, hailed

ACTOR JOSEPH FIENNES PORTRAYED THE BARD IN THE 1998 FILM *SHAKESPEARE IN LOVE*, DIRECTED BY JOHN MADDEN.

Shakespeare as the English Ovid, supreme in love poetry as well as drama. "The Muses would speak with Shakespeare's fine filed phrase," Meres wrote, "if they would speak English." He added praise of Shakespeare's "sugared sonnets among his private friends." It is tantalizing; Meres seems to know something of the poet's personal life, but he gives us no hard information. No wonder biographers are frustrated.

Next the Bard returned gloriously to tragedy with *Julius Caesar*. In the play Caesar has returned to Rome in great popularity after his military triumphs. Brutus and several other leading senators, suspecting that Caesar means to make himself king, plot to assassinate him. Midway through the play, after the assassination, comes one of Shakespeare's most famous scenes. Brutus speaks at Caesar's funeral. But then Caesar's friend Mark Antony delivers a powerful attack on the conspirators, inciting the mob to fury. Brutus and the others, forced to flee Rome, die in the ensuing civil war. In the end the spirit of Caesar wins after all. If Shakespeare had written nothing after *Julius Caesar*, he would still have been remembered as one of the greatest playwrights of all time. But his supreme works were still to come.

Only Shakespeare could have surpassed *Julius Caesar*, and he did so with *Hamlet* (usually dated about 1600). King Hamlet of Denmark has died, apparently bitten by a poisonous snake. Claudius, his brother, has married the dead king's widow, Gertrude, and become the new king, to the disgust and horror of Prince Hamlet. The ghost of old Hamlet appears to young Hamlet, reveals that he was actually poisoned by Claudius, and demands revenge. Hamlet accepts this as his duty, but cannot bring himself to kill his hated uncle. What follows is Shakespeare's most brilliant and controversial plot.

The story of *Hamlet* is set against the religious controversies of the Bard's time. Is the ghost in hell or purgatory? Is Hamlet Catholic or Protestant? Can revenge ever be justified? We are never really given the answers to such questions. But the play reverberates with them.

THE KING'S MEN

In 1603 Queen Elizabeth I died, and King James VI of Scotland became King James I of England. He also became the patron of Shakespeare's acting company, so the Lord Chamberlain's Men became the King's Men. From this point on, we know less of Shakespeare's life in London than in Stratford, where he kept acquiring property.

In the later years of the sixteenth century Shakespeare had been a rather elusive figure in London, delinquent in paying taxes. From 1602 to 1604 he lived, according to his own later testimony, with a French immigrant family named Mountjoy. After 1604 there is no record of any London residence for Shakespeare, nor do we have any reliable recollection of him or his whereabouts by others. As always, the documents leave much to be desired.

Nearly as great as *Hamlet* is *Othello*, and many regard *King Lear*, the heartbreaking tragedy about an old king and his three daughters, as Shakespeare's supreme tragedy. Shakespeare's shortest tragedy, *Macbeth*, tells the story of a Scottish lord and his wife who plot to murder the king of Scotland to gain the throne for themselves. *Antony and Cleopatra*, a sequel to *Julius Caesar*, depicts the aging Mark Antony in love with the enchanting queen of Egypt. *Coriolanus*, another Roman tragedy, is the poet's least popular masterpiece.

SONNETS AND THE END

The year 1609 saw the publication of Shakespeare's Sonnets. Of these 154 puzzling love poems, the first 126 are addressed to a handsome young man, unnamed, but widely believed to be the Earl of Southampton; the rest concern a dark woman, also unidentified. These mysteries are still debated by scholars.

Near the end of his career Shakespeare turned to comedy again, but it was a comedy of a new and more serious kind. Magic plays a large role in these late plays. For example, in *The Tempest*, the exiled duke of Milan, Prospero, uses magic to defeat his enemies and bring about a final reconciliation.

According to the most commonly accepted view, Shakespeare, not yet fifty, retired to Stratford around 1610. He died prosperous in 1616 and left a will that divided his goods, with a famous provision leaving his wife "my second-best bed." He was buried in the chancel of the parish church, under a tombstone bearing a crude rhyme:

> GOOD FRIEND, FOR JESUS SAKE FORBEARE,
> TO DIG THE DUST ENCLOSED HERE.
> BLEST BE THE MAN THAT SPARES THESE STONES,
> AND CURSED BE HE THAT MOVES MY BONES.

This epitaph is another hotly debated mystery: did the great poet actually compose these lines himself?

SHAKESPEARE'S GRAVE IN HOLY TRINITY CHURCH, STRATFORD-UPON-AVON. HIS WIFE, ANNE HATHAWAY, IS BURIED BESIDE HIM.

SHAKESPEARE EXPLAINED: THE TEMPEST

THE FOLIO

In 1623 Shakespeare's colleagues of the King's Men produced a large volume of the plays (excluding the sonnets and other poems) titled *The Comedies, Histories, and Tragedies of Mr. William Shakespeare* with a woodcut portrait—the only known portrait—of the Bard. As a literary monument it is priceless, containing our only texts of half the plays; as a source of biographical information it is severely disappointing, giving not even the dates of Shakespeare's birth and death.

Ben Jonson, then England's poet laureate, supplied a long prefatory poem saluting Shakespeare as the equal of the great classical Greek tragedians Aeschylus, Sophocles, and Euripides, adding that "He was not of an age, but for all time."

Some would later denigrate Shakespeare. His reputation took more than a century to conquer Europe, where many regarded him as semi-barbarous. His works were not translated before 1740. Jonson himself, despite his personal affection, would deprecate "idolatry" of the Bard. For a time Jonson himself was considered more "correct" than Shakespeare, and possibly the superior artist.

But Jonson's generous verdict is now the whole world's. Shakespeare was not merely of his own age, "but for all time."

I WOULD FAIN DIE A DRY DEATH.

A GLOSSARY OF LITERARY TERMS

allegory—a story in which characters and events stand for general moral truths. Shakespeare never uses this form simply, but his plays are full of allegorical elements.

alliteration—repetition of one or more initial sounds, especially consonants, as in the saying "through thick and thin," or in Julius Caesar's statement, "veni, vidi, vici."

allusion—a reference, especially when the subject referred to is not actually named, but is unmistakably hinted at.

aside—a short speech in which a character speaks to the audience, unheard by other characters on the stage.

comedy—a story written to amuse, using devices such as witty dialogue (high comedy) or silly physical movement (low comedy). Most of Shakespeare's comedies were romantic comedies, incorporating lovers who endure separations, misunderstandings, and other obstacles but who are finally united in a happy resolution.

deus ex machina—an unexpected, artificial resolution to a play's convoluted plot. Literally, "god out of a machine."

dialogue—speech that takes place among two or more characters.

diction—choice of words for a given tone. A speech's diction may be dignified (as when a king formally addresses his court), comic (as when the ignorant grave diggers debate whether Ophelia deserves a religious funeral), vulgar, romantic, or whatever the dramatic occasion requires. Shakespeare was a master of diction.

Elizabethan—having to do with the reign of Queen Elizabeth I, from 1558 until her death in 1603. This is considered the most famous period in the history of England, chiefly because of Shakespeare and other noted authors (among them Sir Philip Sidney, Edmund Spenser, and Christopher Marlowe). It was also an era of military glory, especially the defeat of the huge Spanish Armada in 1588.

Globe—the Globe Theater housed Shakespeare's acting company, the Lord Chamberlain's Men (later known as the King's Men). Built in 1598, it caught fire and burned down during a performance of *Henry VIII* in 1613.

hyperbole—an excessively elaborate exaggeration used to create special emphasis or a comic effect, as in Montague's remark that his son Romeo's sighs are "adding to clouds more clouds" in *Romeo and Juliet*.

irony—a discrepancy between what a character says and what he or she truly believes, what is expected to happen and

what really happens, or what a character says
and what others understand.

metaphor—a figure of speech in which one thing is identified
with another, such as when Hamlet calls his father a "fair
mountain." (See also **simile**.)

monologue—a speech delivered by a single character.

motif—a recurrent theme or image, such as disease in *Hamlet*
or moonlight in *A Midsummer Night's Dream*.

oxymoron—a phrase that combines two contradictory terms, as
in the phrase "sounds of silence" or Hamlet's remark, "I must
be cruel only to be kind."

personification—imparting personality to something impersonal
("the sky wept"); giving human qualities to an idea or an
inanimate object, as in the saying "love is blind."

pun—a playful treatment of words that sound alike, or are
exactly the same, but have different meanings. In *Romeo and
Juliet* Mercutio says, after being fatally wounded, "Ask for
me tomorrow and you shall find me a grave man." *Grave* could
mean either "a place of burial" or "serious."

simile—a figure of speech in which one thing is compared to
another, usually using the word *like* or *as*. (See also **metaphor**.)

soliloquy—a speech delivered by a single character, addressed
to the audience. The most famous are those of Hamlet,
but Shakespeare uses this device frequently to tell us his
characters' inner thoughts.

symbol—a visible thing that stands for an invisible quality, as poison in *Hamlet* stands for evil and treachery.

syntax—sentence structure or grammar. Shakespeare displays amazing variety of syntax, from the sweet simplicity of his songs to the clotted fury of his great tragic heroes, who can be very difficult to understand at a first hearing. These effects are deliberate; if we are confused, it is because Shakespeare means to confuse us.

theme—the abstract subject or message of a work of art, such as revenge in *Hamlet* or overweening ambition in *Macbeth*.

tone—the style or approach of a work of art. The tone of *A Midsummer Night's Dream*, set by the lovers, Bottom's crew, and the fairies, is light and sweet. The tone of *Macbeth*, set by the witches, is dark and sinister.

tragedy—a story that traces a character's fall from power, sanity, or privilege. Shakespeare's well-known tragedies include *Hamlet, Macbeth,* and *Othello*.

tragicomedy—a story that combines elements of both tragedy and comedy, moving a heavy plot through twists and turns to a happy ending.

verisimilitude—having the appearance of being real or true.

understatement—a statement expressing less than intended, often with an ironic or comic intention; the opposite of hyperbole.

SHAKESPEARE AND
THE TEMPEST

JOSEPH M
SCHENCK
PRESENTS

A movie poster features ▶
Camilla Horn and John
Barrymore in a 1928 United
Artists film, *Tempest.*

JOHN BARR

"TEMPEST"

66929 66929

Shakespeare and *The Tempest*

CHAPTER ONE

THE TEMPEST WAS THE LAST PLAY THAT WAS ENTIRELY SHAKESPEARE'S OWN AND HAS OFTEN BEEN INTERPRETED AS SHAKESPEARE'S FAREWELL TO THE THEATER. THIS CAN BE DEBATED. **THE TEMPEST** IS VERY MUCH OF THE MOMENT IN WHICH IT WAS WRITTEN. IT DRAWS ON CONTEMPORARY EVENTS, MOST NOTABLY THE LOSS OF A SHIP IN "A DREADFUL TEMPEST" EN ROUTE TO THE STRUGGLING COLONY AT JAMESTOWN, VIRGINIA, IN 1609. AND IT CONTINUES THE EXPERIMENTATION OF SHAKESPEARE'S LATE WORK, INCORPORATING THE POSSIBILITIES AFFORDED BY NEW GENRES AND NEW THEATRICAL VENUES AND TECHNOLOGIES.

The Tempest does have the sense of being a culminating work in Shakespeare's career. Through the story of the powerful magician Prospero, whose art—magic—represents learning, ingenuity, and technology, but also theater, Shakespeare explores the ability of using theater to enforce a vision and create a world. More surprisingly, perhaps, Shakespeare links these questions concerning power and projection in the theater to events and questions raised by the project of English plantation in the New World at the time the play was written and first performed—sometimes for an audience that would have included stockholders and potential investors in the Virginia Company.

By the time *The Tempest* was written, Shakespeare's plays were being performed in three different venues: the Globe, the court of James I, and Blackfriars, an indoor theater that Shakespeare's company acquired in 1608. Having an indoor theater meant that Shakespeare's company could perform plays in the winter and at night (by candlelight), which they could not do in the outdoor theater of the Globe. This allowed the use of softer musical instruments (woodwinds rather than brass) and provided new possibilities for set design and stage machinery. Blackfriars also served a smaller audience that was able to pay higher admission prices.

King James I was an avid supporter of theater, and several topics taken up in *The Tempest* have been linked to James's specific interests: magic and witchcraft, the question of the duties of a ruler, the issue of absolute power, and dynastic political marriages.

But James also fostered theatrical productions of a different kind. This was the age of opulent "masques" at James's court: expensive multimedia productions with poetry, music, dancing, and spectacular sets and costumes designed by the foremost poets and artisans of the age. The masques produced for King James were celebrations of the triumph of order over disorder, representations of cosmic and social harmony confirming the centrality and authority of the king as absolute monarch. The masques and the new indoor plays regularly used music and spectacle as vehicles of meaning. Most simply, but crucially, this means that when we read the text of *The Tempest* on the page, we must read the stage directions. Some of the most important things that happen in the play happen as spectacle during which nothing is spoken.

The masques also prepare us to expect a symbolic use of characters and setting. In *The Tempest*, allegorical and symbolic elements abound. The island on which the action of the play takes place is itself both a literal and a symbolic space. It is an island in the Mediterranean Sea; it is a place of projection where different people see different things; it stands for the New World; it is a symbol for the bare stage. Once we are alerted to the possibilities that this symbolic space opens up, the island goes a long way toward helping us integrate the layers of meaning in the play—and toward understanding why this very short play, in which very little seems to happen, has had so extensive a reach in four hundred years of interpretation.

It is often said that *The Tempest* has the rare plot for which Shakespeare had no source. The more accurate way to put this might be to say that scholars have discovered too *many* possible sources to settle on just one, and that none tells the complete story. For example, Prospero's speech in which he gives up magic is adapted from a speech by Medea in Ovid's *Metamorphoses* (in Golding's 1567 translation). Gonzalo speaks words from Montaigne's essay "Of the Cannibals" in Act II. To these literary sources must be added a set of writings related to travel, exploration, and the fledgling English attempts at colonization in the New World. A special case is presented by the documents connected to a contemporary event: the wreck of a ship called the *Sea Venture* off the coast of Bermuda in 1609.

On June 2, 1609, a fleet of nine ships set sail for the Jamestown Colony in Virginia with the newly appointed governor of the colony. On July 24 they were beset by a hurricane: "a most dreadful tempest," during which the ship bearing 150 men, women, and children was given up for lost. It was learned nearly a year later, however, that the ship had miraculously—or providentially—wrecked on the rocks off the Bermudas, then known and much feared as the Isle of Devils. The islands turned out to be a hospitable island paradise. The colonists survived the winter well fed and in good health, and nine months later, with two rebuilt vessels, they made it to Jamestown.

At least three accounts of the wreck and its aftermath are believed

EDMUND DULAC'S 1908
PAINTING, THE WRECK,
FROM "THE TEMPEST"

to have been known to Shakespeare. He is said to have taken specific details about the storm from these accounts: details about seafaring and the behavior of those aboard the sinking ship; the cask of beer thrown overboard; physical details about the island and its wildlife; and the whole idea of a providential rescue, which is expanded upon at length by Gonzalo in *The Tempest.*

What to make of these connections has been the source of much debate. Some scholars have simply used the Virginia references to date when the play was written: 1610–1611. Others have read the play as an allegorical representation of Europeans in the New World. Still others have opened up the play to a wider investigation of the history and discourses of colonialism and slavery, with contexts ranging from the Caribbean to Africa to Ireland.

Finally, *The Tempest* is the last of four late plays we call the romances: *Pericles* (1608), *The Winter's Tale* (1609), *Cymbeline* (1610), and *The Tempest* (1611). The term *romance* was first assigned to these late plays by Edward Dowden in 1875; in Shakespeare's time, the theatrical genre was called "tragie-comedie," and the Folio lists *The Tempest* as a comedy.

But the four plays have certain things in common, among them sea voyages and shipwrecks; improbable, if not supernatural, rescues and resolutions; central father-daughter relationships; and themes of loss and recovery, forgiveness and reconciliation. The new genre, with its hybrid of tragedy and comedy, also brought a new openness to techniques and motifs adapted from narrative romances and novellas, including the supernatural. The romances are among Shakespeare's most experimental plays. They all take advantage of Blackfriars theater, and they all experiment with time, representation, the relationship between storytelling and dramatic representation, and the limits of probability onstage.

Formally *The Tempest* is at once the most tightly structured and the most wide open of the romances. It observes the unities of time and space. All that happened before the play began is narrated in Act I, Scene 2, as back story. The time of the play's action—between the hours of 2:00 P.M. and 6:00 P.M.—is then nearly matched by the performance time, and with the exception of the storm, everything takes place on the island.

At the same time *The Tempest* incorporates many kinds of material in a diversity of inserted genres, and the play is open to multiple interpretive possibilities. We're safely on the island, but the island is at once in the Mediterranean and near Bermuda, and it is impossible to describe the island in such a way that everyone will agree that they are seeing the same thing. The boundaries between nature and art, illusion and reality, are both used and rendered uncertain.

Thematically *The Tempest* is a romance in the sense that previous wrongs are ultimately made good, and reconciliation is achieved by means of forgiveness. But part of how this happens in *The Tempest* is that the magician Prospero *stages* a romance. And not everything fits. Antonio and Sebastian do not repent. Caliban is a loose end, left with no certain future and no ideal place to go. Prospero's own struggles are often on the margins of the romance that he stages. And perhaps most important, although it is magic that Prospero uses to stage the romance, it is precisely that magic— his "so potent Art"—that Prospero gives up at the end of the play. Read through to its conclusion, this would make *The Tempest* a romance about giving up romance. Shakespeare's "farewell to the theater" makes us look at the very conditions that make theater possible.

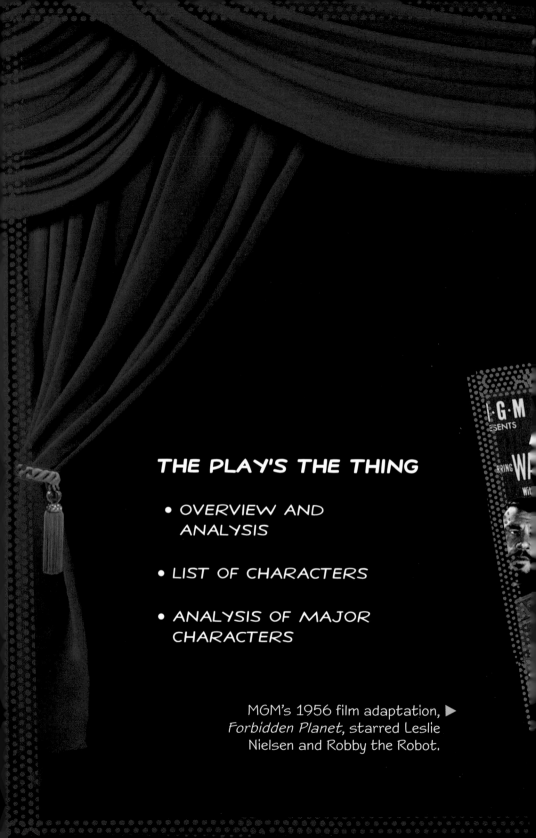

THE PLAY'S THE THING

- OVERVIEW AND ANALYSIS

- LIST OF CHARACTERS

- ANALYSIS OF MAJOR CHARACTERS

MGM's 1956 film adaptation, ▶
Forbidden Planet, starred Leslie
Nielsen and Robby the Robot.

Chapter One

CHAPTER TWO

The Play's the Thing

OVERVIEW

The Tempest begins on a ship about to go down in a terrifying storm. On board, besides the ship's crew, are Alonso, the king of Naples, and his court. The ship's master and the boatswain are trying to save the ship, and the boatswain is frustrated by the interference of the royal passengers. Admonished to show more respect for the king, the boatswain retorts that the storm cares nothing for "the name of king." If their authority can stop the storm, then let them use it. If not, they should get out of the way.

The king's counselor Gonzalo, perpetually optimistic, suggests that the insolent boatswain was born to be hanged on dry land, in which case they might all survive the storm. Sebastian, the king's brother, and Antonio, the duke of Milan, curse and complain. The scene ends with the mariners in despair about whether they will be able to save the ship—"We split, we split!"—and our expectation is that everyone aboard will drown.

ANALYSIS

The scene puts us in the middle of a storm so powerful that it challenges the human social order. In response to the question "Where is the master?" the boatswain answers, "Do you not hear him?" The storm is the master here. Nature is more powerful than human hierarchy.

The extreme circumstances of the storm introduce us quickly to the temperament and qualities of the king's followers. Gonzalo is loyal, protective of the social order, and optimistic. Antonio and Sebastian are aggressive, insulting, and ready to curse: "A pox o' your throat, you bawling, blasphemous, incharitable dog!"

The boatswain (pronounced "bo'sun") is the ship's officer in charge of the sails, the masts, and the men who man them. He is competent, pragmatic, and—in this life-and-death situation—as unimpressed with the trappings of royalty as is the sea.

ACT I, SCENE 2

OVERVIEW

The action shifts to an island from which the magician Prospero and his daughter Miranda watch the ship "dashed all to pieces." Miranda guesses immediately that her father has caused the storm and the destruction of the ship, and she is horrified. She identifies with the suffering she sees, and says that if such godlike power had been hers, she would have stopped it.

But Prospero insists that no one has been harmed. He takes off his magic robes and says that the entire "spectacle of the wreck" was under the control of his magic. He then proceeds to tell her why he has caused

PROSPERO (ALVIN EPSTEIN), UNCLOAKED, TELLS MIRANDA (MARA SIDMORE) OF HIS MAGICAL POWERS IN THE BOSTON ACTORS' SHAKESPEARE PROJECT'S 2008 PRODUCTION.

the storm, which requires him to tell her the story of their true identities and history.

This is something that Prospero has started to tell Miranda before, but he has always broken off without finishing. Now Prospero explains that, until twelve years earlier, he had been the duke of Milan, both "a prince of power" and a scholar "without a parallel." Unfortunately he had put the job of managing the dukedom into the hands of his brother, Antonio, so that that he could spend all his time on his studies. Antonio staged a coup with the help of the king of Naples, Alonso, and Prospero and his two-year-old daughter Miranda were put out to sea in a rickety little boat. They survived "by providence divine," but also because "the good Gonzalo" had provided them with provisions and with Prospero's books, the source of his magic power: "Knowing I loved my books, he furnished me / From mine own library with volumes that / I prize above my dukedom." The present tense is important here: He says "prize," not "prized." Prospero still prizes his books above his dukedom.

Prospero explains that he raised the storm because his reading of the stars had informed him that his enemies, Alonso and Antonio, had come within his reach, and that he had to act now or lose his chance forever. He then puts Miranda to sleep and calls his servant Ariel.

Ariel is the spirit who does Prospero's bidding and enacts his commands. We learn that it was Ariel who "performed" the tempest and "flamed amazement" on the ship. Ariel informs Prospero that everyone but the mariners jumped overboard in terror, and that Ariel has dispersed them in groups about the island. Ferdinand, the king's son, is alone. The mariners are sleeping under a spell inside the ship, which Ariel has hidden "in the deep nook where once / Thou called'st me up at midnight to fetch dew / From the still-vexed Bermoothes." It is 2:00 P.M., and Prospero expects their work to be done by 6:00 P.M.

Ariel reminds Prospero that he promised Ariel his (or her) liberty, and Prospero, angry, recaps the story of how Ariel came to serve him. Ariel had been imprisoned in a pine tree by a powerful witch named Sycorax, who had been banished to the island from Algiers when she was pregnant. Sycorax could not undo the spell, and Ariel remained trapped in the pine

ARIEL (GILZ TERERA) AND PROSPERO
(PHILIP VOSS) IN THE ROYAL SHAKESPEARE
COMPANY'S 2000 PRODUCTION

for twelve years. During that time Sycorax died, leaving no other "human shape" on the island except Caliban, the son she bore. When Prospero arrived, he was able to free Ariel from the pine. Now Prospero threatens to imprison Ariel again, this time in an oak, if Ariel keeps complaining, and

Ariel is once more compliant. Prospero gives Ariel further instructions, telling him to remain invisible to all eyes but Prospero's.

Prospero wakes Miranda and tells her they must visit Caliban, who is now Prospero's slave. Miranda would prefer to avoid the meeting, but Prospero says they need Caliban for their menial work. Prospero insults Caliban from the beginning, calling him dirt ("Thou earth"), tortoise (because he is slow), poisonous, and "got by the devil himself." (This last comment is sometimes interpreted literally; others see it as just one more insult from Prospero.) Caliban curses both Prospero and Miranda. Prospero responds with promises of cramps and other tortures.

As the conversation continues, we learn that this intense hostility is fueled by resentment and disappointment on both sides. When Prospero first arrived on the island, Caliban showed him the secrets of the island and how to survive, and Prospero took Caliban into his household and undertook his education. By both accounts, this continued until Caliban tried to rape Miranda. Now Caliban is physically confined away from the living quarters they used to share. Caliban views his imprisonment and enslavement as an extension of Prospero's usurpation of the island he inherited from his mother. Prospero and Miranda focus on the attempted rape, which they view as a betrayal of the care they devoted to Caliban's education. Caliban does not deny the rape attempt, and regrets only that it did not succeed. Miranda responds angrily, reminding him that she

"GOOD WOMBS HAVE BORNE BAD SONS."

had pitied him and taught him language. But Caliban retorts, "You taught me language, and my profit on't / Is I know how to curse." They speak at cross-purposes here. Both are bitter, neither acknowledges the other's grievance, and the conflict is unresolved. Prospero sends Caliban off to fetch firewood.

Now Ariel, visible only to Prospero, brings on Ferdinand, the son of King Alonso. Ferdinand believes his father has drowned. Ariel lures him on with music, which Ferdinand says has both comforted him and stilled the fury of the waves. Ariel's second song offers Ferdinand a haunting vision of his dead father, transformed by the sea ("Full fathom five . . .").

Prospero reveals Ferdinand to Miranda, speaking as if her eyelashes were the curtains of a stage. She sees Ferdinand as "a thing divine," and Prospero has to convince her that anything so beautiful could be human. Ferdinand has the same reaction when he sees Miranda, mistaking her for a goddess. Prospero has brought them together in the hope that they will fall in love, and they do; but Prospero pretends to mistrust Ferdinand and to forbid the relationship in order to keep the prize of love from appearing too easily won. Prospero imprisons Ferdinand, but Ferdinand doesn't care, so long as he can see Miranda. Miranda stands up for Ferdinand and is rebuked by Prospero, but she is undaunted and quietly tells Ferdinand not to be too bothered by Prospero's behavior.

HOW TO NAME THE BIGGER LIGHT AND HOW THE LESS.

Scene 2 is the longest one in the play, and it breaks down into four separate conversations or encounters. The first three—which are conversations between Prospero and Miranda; Prospero and Ariel; and then Prospero, Miranda, and Caliban—fill in part of the history of what happened before the start of the play. The fourth encounter—with Ferdinand—takes the action forward.

The very first moment of Scene 2 is of vital importance, because it immediately causes us to reinterpret everything we have just seen on stage. The tempest of the first scene introduced us to the overwhelming power of nature. Neither the ship nor the conventions of human society was equal to the force of the storm. Now this nature turns out to have been entirely under the control of Prospero's art. The borderline between art and nature has been put into question, and the power of each is being contested.

Next, Prospero and Miranda appear onstage as spectators, watching the same scene we just watched. We are reminded for the first of many times that this play is not only about magic but also about watching theater. Miranda is a model spectator, not only in her attentiveness but also in her compassionate response. When she says, "I have suffered / with those that I saw suffer," she gives the exact etymology of the word *compassion*, which means "to suffer with." Note, however, that Miranda's first response to Prospero's "Tell your piteous heart / There's no harm done" is "woe the day": We learn that Miranda believes that her father is capable not only of taking the lives of those on board the ship but also of telling her *not* to feel pity for their suffering. The virtue of compassion comes much more easily to Miranda than it does to her father.

Prospero's narrative of the story of his life contains some of the most difficult language in the play. He interrupts himself with so many digressions and qualifying statements that his meaning can be hard to pick out. If we look for the actual subjects and verbs of these tortuous sentences, however, we begin to find a motive. Prospero wants to present himself as an innocent victim, but he has to tell a story in which he, too, is culpable.

We learn, first, that Prospero neglected his duties as duke while he pursued his studies. This is contrary to the classical ethic of statesmanship that was widely held during the Renaissance, which said that a prince should study only to the extent that it would help him rule.

Second, Prospero became "rapt in secret studies." One of the much-debated questions in the play is whether Prospero is purely a theurgist, a "white magician" (a Neoplatonist mage seeking the highest knowledge of things invisible and leaving the base material world behind), or whether Prospero's magic has crossed over into the dark arts. For most of the play, Prospero works hard to portray his art as the opposite of the witchcraft of Sycorax. Shakespeare's interest may be less in the clash of devils and duty than in the line he inserts in between: "and to my state grew stranger." Prospero grew to be a stranger not only to his political state, his dukedom, but also to his human state. If Prospero was indeed "climbing a ladder to the sky," at the end of the play he will step down a few rungs and rejoin his fellow humans.

The conversation with Ariel begins with Prospero's delight at Ariel's performance, but quickly turns to anger when Ariel seeks liberty. Prospero is eager to portray himself as the opposite of Sycorax, but their stories are also obviously parallel. Both practice magic; both were exiled to the island with a young child. For both, the significant time period is twelve years. This gives us important information about the time frame of the play. It is possible that Sycorax was on the island some time before imprisoning Ariel, but the earliest possible calculation would have Prospero arriving on the island when Caliban was twelve and Miranda just short of three.

DOMINIC LETTS PLAYED CALIBAN AT LONDON'S YOUNG VIC THEATER IN 1995.

This means that when the play starts, Caliban is at least twenty-four, and Miranda is just short of her fifteenth birthday.

Caliban is set up from the beginning as Ariel's counterpart and opposite. Both serve Prospero, and both want freedom. But Ariel is associated with air and Caliban is imprisoned in a rock, and his entry, either from a cave or from a trapdoor underground, emphasizes that he is earthbound in a way that Ariel is not. Ariel is also said to have been "a spirit too delicate / To

"HELL IS EMPTY AND ALL THE DEVILS ARE HERE."

act [the] earthy and abhorred commands" of Sycorax; Caliban is associated with bestiality because of the attempted rape.

The exchange between Miranda and Caliban is important both for what it tells us about the larger themes of the play and for what we see in the encounter between two people whom Prospero has, in a sense, raised. Miranda is angry at Caliban's unrepentant glee as he brags about his attempt to rape her: "O ho, O ho! Would't had been done! / . . . I had peopled else / This isle with Calibans." We do not know when this occurred, but given Miranda's age (she is not yet fifteen), and the freshness of her anger, it may have been very recent. Miranda's speech is so forceful, and its insults so aggressive, that for many years some editors assigned the speech to Prospero instead of Miranda. That is probably giving Miranda too little credit. Caliban has betrayed her trust, her compassion, and her investment in educating him. She admits that Caliban did, in fact, learn, even as she blames his behavior on an intrinsically vile nature. Still, her anger spills over into insults that do indeed sound like Prospero's. Miranda is her father's daughter—and his prize pupil.

Caliban's answer responds not to her grievance, but to the insults, and to her assumption that the language she taught him was a gift: "You taught me language, and my profit on't / Is I know how to curse." The play does not resolve the question of whether Caliban's "gabble" was a language Miranda simply did not understand, or whether Caliban was too young when Sycorax died for him to have learned his mother's language at all. But it captures all of Caliban's bitterness at being schooled to fluency in a language that, for the moment at least, can only underline his lack of status and power.

In contrast to Caliban, Ferdinand expresses himself in the all conventions of romance. Ferdinand and Miranda idealize one another, and the island appears as a place where objects of extreme idealization (and extreme degradation) appear to be real. Perhaps the purest expression of romance conventions is Miranda's certainty that because Ferdinand is beautiful, he must be virtuous as well: "There's nothing ill can dwell in such a temple."

Prospero, who has set up this meeting, pretends to disapprove and treats Ferdinand as a traitor and a threat. Some interpreters of the play have seen this as truer than Prospero realizes, since Ferdinand will indeed replace Prospero in his daughter's affections. But Prospero also has a political purpose in fostering this relationship: if Miranda marries Ferdinand and becomes queen of Naples, Naples and Milan will be united and Miranda's children, Prospero's grandchildren, will be heirs to both.

ACT II, SCENE 1

OVERVIEW

Act 2 begins with the weary king and his party on the island. Alonso is mourning the loss of Ferdinand, who he believes has drowned. We learn that Alonso and his party were on the Mediterranean Sea returning from having married Alonso's daughter Claribel to the king of Tunis in North Africa when the storm struck. We also learn that everyone sees the island differently. Gonzalo and the courtier Adrian see the island as lush, green, fragrant, and providing everything they need to live. Antonio and Sebastian see it as barren, brown ("tawny"), and stinking like a rotten swamp.

Gonzalo seeks to comfort and divert the king, and Antonio and Sebastian amuse themselves by mocking Gonzalo. After confusing modern Tunis and classical Carthage, Gonzalo muses about what he would do if the island were his to colonize ("Had I plantation of this isle . . ."). He says he would make a world of perfect innocence, without the need for labor, agriculture, or sovereignty. "And yet he would be king on't," comments Sebastian. Gonzalo continues with his vision but is dismissed by the weary Alonso.

Ariel arrives and puts all the party to sleep except Antonio and Sebastian. While the others sleep, Antonio persuades Sebastian that they should murder Alonso and Gonzalo so that Sebastian can be king of Naples. Just as they are about to commit the murders, however, Ariel wakes Gonzalo, naming the "open-eyed conspiracy." Antonio and Sebastian pretend that their swords were drawn to kill wild animals.

ANALYSIS

We learn important new information about the island in this scene. First, not everyone sees the island the same way. The island is a place of projection. Here people seem to see according to their characters. The optimistic Gonzalo sees the island as a green, fertile place supporting life, and he notes that everyone's garments are all fresh and undamaged by the sea. Antonio and Sebastian, who have been inclined to mock Gonzalo and curse their deprivation from the beginning, see the island as barren, and they tell Gonzalo to check his pockets to see how fresh their garments really are (implying that theirs are wet and soiled). There is no agreement about the basic empirical facts.

Second, we are given a lesson in the geography of the play. Alonso and his party are returning from Tunis to Naples, which reinforces the location of the island in the Mediterranean Sea. But the fact that the island is both a geographical and a fictional space is reinforced in the banter among Gonzalo, Antonio, and Sebastian about Carthage, Tunis, Aeneas, and Dido (from Virgil's *Aeneid*). History, geography, and legend are confused and overlaid. Gonzalo's misperception, Antonio and Sebastian imply, can create whole cities out of nothing. But this is not so far from the truth: art *can* create fictional space. Moreover, while Prospero's island is a place where history and geography are explicitly subject to magic, by the end of the play, the island itself will serve as an emblem of the stage, and the stage as an emblem of the world itself.

The banter contains another speech that has serious implications. Gonzalo describes the utopia he would establish if he were colonizing the island. He says he would "with such perfection govern, sir, / T'excel the Golden Age." The Golden Age was a mythic era of natural perfection before the intervention of death, seasons, agriculture, cities, civilizations, laws, and government. Shakespeare takes the language of Gonzalo's speech from Montaigne's essay "Of the Cannibals" and from Ovid's *Metamorphoses,* both of which he knew very well. But Shakespeare zeroes in on the contradictions of Gonzalo's utopia. Gonzalo wants to make a perfect world without kings, but he needs to be king in order to create that world.

Finally, when Antonio plots with Sebastian, we watch him engineer a coup that recalls his coup against Prospero twelve years earlier. Sebastian notices this, saying, "I remember / You did supplant your brother Prospero." Antonio is up to the same old tricks, using another person to gain power, and he cheerfully reports that he has no conscience. This time, however, Prospero has matters in hand. It is Ariel who has put the other characters to sleep, and drowsiness infuses the speeches. Dreams, desire, and the

"HE RECEIVES COMFORT LIKE COLD PORRIDGE."

imagination are linked to power and possibility in a pun on the word *might*: "What might, / Worthy Sebastian, O what might—?" We are reminded that Antonio is a virtuoso in the art of political seduction, setting subjects "to what tune pleased his ear."

ACT II, SCENE 2

OVERVIEW

On another part of the island Caliban enters carrying a load of wood and cursing Prospero. Hearing thunder, and anticipating punishment from Prospero's spirits, Caliban sees Trinculo (Alonso's jester) and believes that Trinculo is a spirit sent by Prospero to torment him. Caliban hides under his cloak. Trinculo, seeking shelter from the storm, crawls under Caliban's cloak as well. Comedy ensues. Caliban thinks he's being tormented by a spirit, and when Stephano (Alonso's butler) staggers in drunk, he thinks he has found a four-legged, two-headed monster. He pours liquor into both mouths, recognizes Trinculo, and wonders at Caliban, whom he calls a "mooncalf": a monstrosity born under the influence of the moon. Caliban, in awe of the "celestial liquor," mistakes Stephano for a god: "Hast thou not dropped from heaven?" He offers Stephano his services, continuing to idealize him ("thou wondrous man"). Trinculo finds this ridiculous and says so, but, convinced that they are the only survivors of the wreck, Stephano is quite cheerfully prepared to inherit the island. Now drunk, Caliban sings a song of freedom from Prospero, although he has chosen a new master in Stephano.

ANALYSIS

This comic scene also presents some of the most important issues in the play, among them what exactly is human, animal, or "monster." When Trinculo sees Caliban's strangeness, he recalls freak shows in England where people who won't give a dime to a beggar will pay a dollar to see "a

CALIBAN (GEFF FRANCIS, CENTER) LABORS RESENTFULLY, AS ARIEL (KANANU KIRIMI, RIGHT) STANDS BY, IN THE ROYAL SHAKESPEARE COMPANY'S 2002 PRODUCTION.

dead Indian." Looking more closely, however, Trinculo recognizes that the monster's "fins" are, in fact, arms, and he concludes that "this is no fish, but an islander." Trinculo also comments that back in England, "there would this monster make a man." "Make a man" has at least two meanings. Having a monster to exhibit for money would make a man's fortune. But it also means that, in England, a monster can pass for a man, and perhaps many who pass for men are indeed "monsters."

Caliban's wonder at Stephano recalls the wonder of Miranda when she first saw Ferdinand (and Ferdinand when he first saw Miranda). Caliban's promise to show Stephano the best spots on the island also repeats what he did when Prospero first arrived. We understand that Stephano is less worthy an object of wonder than Miranda, but there is also an element of parody here. Like Prospero, Stephano says he will "give [Caliban] language," but he does so by pouring liquor into his mouth. So, too, Stephano refers to his bottle as his "book," recalling Prospero's book, although the "spirits" at Stephano's command are his "celestial liquor."

ACT III, SCENE 1

OVERVIEW

At Prospero's cell Ferdinand enters, carrying a log. Miranda regrets that he is doing menial work, but Ferdinand is secure in the knowledge that "some kinds of baseness / Are nobly undergone." Besides, he serves for love. Ferdinand and Miranda confess their love for one another, each offering the other service. Miranda proposes marriage ("Hence, bashful cunning, / And prompt me, plain and holy innocence!"), and Ferdinand pledges himself "with a heart as willing / As bondage e'er of freedom." They exchange hands and are betrothed. Prospero watches and is pleased.

ANALYSIS

Ferdinand's entry, carrying a log, is a visual echo of Caliban's entrance in the previous scene. Again we have a parallel, and also a distinct contrast. Ferdinand has taken Caliban's place, to the extent that he is shackled and forced to do menial work. But the fact that Ferdinand chooses to interpret this as service to Miranda allows him to transfigure the labor into something tolerable and even noble. Ferdinand's respect and restraint also contrast sharply with Caliban's assault on Miranda. There is, in fact, plenty of desire in this scene, and Miranda says that she will die if she

FERDINAND (OLIVER DIMSDALE) VOWS TO MARRY MIRANDA (NIKKI AMUKA-BIRD) IN THE ROYAL SHAKESPEARE COMPANY'S 2000 PRODUCTION.

does not get Ferdinand. But the love of Ferdinand and Miranda is mutual, and their desire to serve one another is reciprocal. The overwhelming impression we get is a mix of innocence, candor, and purpose.

Prospero calls down a blessing on the lovers and "that which breeds between them." This is in the first instance their love, but the marriage of Ferdinand and Miranda will unite Naples and Milan. And their children, Prospero's grandchildren, will inherit both.

OVERVIEW

Caliban, Trinculo, and Stephano are still drinking. Stephano has adopted Caliban as his "servant-monster," but Caliban plays the role of courtier instead, treating Stephano as his would-be king: "Wilt thou be pleased to hearken once again to the suit I made to thee?" The "suit" is a plot for Stephano to murder Prospero and become king of the island.

The invisible Ariel makes trouble between Trinculo and Stephano, mimicking both of their voices to each other to provoke them to fight. Stephano agrees to murder Prospero, however, and declares that he and Miranda will rule as king and queen, and Trinculo and Caliban will be his viceroys.

To celebrate, Caliban asks Trinculo and Stephano to sing a particular song that he likes, but he is disappointed by the drunken song they sing instead. Ariel (still invisible) plays the music Caliban wanted to hear. Stephano and Trinculo panic, terrified at the music "played by the picture of Nobody." But Caliban comforts them in what is arguably the most lyrical speech of the play: "Be not afeard. The isle is full of noises, / Sounds, and sweet airs, that give delight and hurt not. . . ."

Stephano looks forward to having his music for nothing when he is king. Caliban reminds him that this will happen only "when Prospero is destroyed."

ANALYSIS

In language and gesture, Caliban's plot parallels Antonio's plot to enlist Sebastian as conspirator in the murder of Alonso (after which Antonio will serve Sebastian as king). Now Caliban enlists Stephano as conspirator in the murder of Prospero (after which he will serve Stephano as king). The second parallel is with Antonio's original usurpation of Prospero's

MISERY ACQUAINTS A MAN WITH STRANGE BEDFELLOWS."

dukedom. The plan is for them to strike while Prospero is asleep in his study, having first seized his books. Caliban has become Antonio's double.

The scene also shows another side of Caliban, however. The "Sounds, and sweet airs, that give delight and hurt not" have particular poignancy as the opposite of Prospero's cramps and pinches: here Caliban recalls only beauty and delight. Caliban's speech evokes all the longing of desire, and dreams as the imagined fulfillment of desire, if only in sleep. But the speech also shows us a different side of Caliban as a speaker: linguistically adept, poetic, cultured, and at the furthest extreme from cursing. The speech is a vital piece of the puzzle that is Caliban, and any interpretation of Caliban must contend with the fact that Shakespeare has given him some of the best poetry in the play.

ACT III, SCENE 3

OVERVIEW

As Alonso and his courtiers continue to wander on the island, Prospero's spirits bring out a banquet for them. They are amazed to see these "monstrous shapes," and they suddenly believe in the truth of all the imaginary creatures they have ever read about. Gonzalo observes the spirits' gentle manners, however, and persuades the king to eat the food they have laid out. Suddenly the banquet is interrupted by the terrible spectacle of Ariel in the form of a Harpy—a mythological monster that is half woman and half bird of prey. Ariel (as the Harpy) accuses Alonso,

ARIEL (SCOTT HANDY) DESCENDS AS A HARPY WITH PROSPERO (DAVID CALDER) IN THE FOREGROUND IN THE ROYAL SHAKESPEARE COMPANY'S 1998 PRODUCTION.

Antonio, and Sebastian of their crime in deposing Prospero and claims that the seas, now serving fate, have taken their revenge. More pointedly Ariel tells Alonso that the loss of his son Ferdinand has been direct punishment for his crime, and that he is doomed to a lifetime of suffering unless he repents and changes his life. Alonso, struck with remorse, runs off at the end of the scene to commit suicide by drowning. Antonio and Sebastian, also crazed, draw their swords and run off to fight "fiends."

Gonzalo has not heard the Harpy's words: "I'th'name of something holy, sir, why stand you / In this strange stare?" Yet from what Alonso has said, and from the reactions of Antonio and Sebastian, Gonzalo infers that they are struck by guilt. We are reminded that Gonzalo was witness to the original crime of deposing Prospero.

Prospero is thrilled with Ariel's performance and its effect. He congratulates himself that his enemies are now mad ("knit up / In their distractions"). He leaves them that way and goes to visit Ferdinand and Miranda.

ANALYSIS

The third and final scene of Act III presents us with a climax, insofar as the plot of the play has to do with Prospero's triumph over his enemies and his ability to get his dukedom back. Prospero has staged the conditions for Alonso's repentance: Alonso has been grieving the death of Ferdinand, and now that he believes he is responsible for that death, he is struck by remorse. Alonso's repentance ultimately depends on his character, however. Antonio, who has no conscience, is crazed but not chastened by what the Harpy has said.

Alonso's moment of recognition is captured in his declaration, "O, it is monstrous, monstrous!" The description fits the Harpy and the terrible vision, but in the rest of the speech the term is applied to his own crime. What Alonso did with his royal powers was worse than what would be done in nature, and in this sense, it is "monstrous." In other parts of the play the term *monster* has been applied to Caliban, presumably because of some kind of physical deformity; but here the word *monstrous* is applied to moral deformity, and to moral deformity in a king. The hyperbole of the word *monstrous* may also take Alonso too far, however, for he has gone past repentance to despair.

ACT IV, SCENE 1

OVERVIEW

Prospero tells Ferdinand that his harsh treatment was only a test of Ferdinand's worthiness to win his prized and most beloved daughter. Ferdinand has passed the test, and Prospero formally gives him Miranda to be his wife. Miranda does not speak, but we assume that she is pleased with the outcome. After strenuous warnings about not giving way to lust before the marriage has taken place, Prospero releases the lovers to sit and talk at will.

Prospero then calls on Ariel to gather the spirits: he wants to show the lovers "Some vanity of [his] art."

The spirits, playing goddesses, put on a wedding masque. Prospero watches with Ferdinand and Miranda as Iris (the rainbow) calls Ceres (goddess of the earth's fertility) and Juno (goddess of marriage) to bless the marriage. Ceres makes sure that Venus won't be coming (lust is to be kept at bay); Juno arrives by chariot from the sky. Juno and Ceres sing their blessings of honor, riches, joy, and plenty.

In answer to a question from Ferdinand, Prospero confirms that they are watching spirits whom Prospero has summoned to act out his wishes. Ferdinand is impressed, and declares his wish that he could live in this paradise forever.

The masque continues. Iris summons nymphs from their rivers, and they are then joined in dancing by sunburned reapers from the fields. Suddenly, unexpectedly, Prospero stops the show. The stage direction tells us that "Prospero starts suddenly and speaks, after which, to a strange hollow and confused noise, they heavily vanish."

Prospero's explanation is that he had forgotten the conspiracy of Caliban. Ferdinand and Miranda are concerned. Miranda has never seen him so upset, and Ferdinand wonders at the force of whatever emotion has him in its grip. Prospero seeks to comfort what he sees as Ferdinand's dismay by reminding him that the whole masque was, after all, a fiction acted by spirits, a vision without substance. And he tells him that the whole world, and everyone in it, will disappear just as completely someday. He sends Ferdinand and Miranda inside, and then calls Ariel: "Spirit, we must prepare to meet with Caliban."

Ariel already has Caliban, Trinculo, and Stephano under control. He reports that he has lured them through briars and into a stinking pond. Prospero now instructs Ariel to put out "trumpery"—fancy clothes— as bait.

While Ariel is gone, Prospero stews about his failures with Caliban. Ariel brings out the fancy clothes and hangs them up. Upon entering, Trinculo and Stephano immediately start dressing up, but Caliban is not amused: "Let it alone, thou fool, it is but trash." But they pile clothes onto him— their "servant-monster." Prospero and Ariel send spirits after them in the form of hunting dogs, and Prospero's last commands are for more tortures. The scene ends with Prospero's declaration that all his enemies are now completely at his mercy.

ANALYSIS

In Act IV, Prospero takes the opportunity to show off his art. The masque that his spirits present is a play within the play, and Prospero, Ferdinand, and Miranda watch as spectators. The goddesses (played by Ariel and other spirits) present a perfect world without winter and offer the lovers the blessings of a happy marriage and healthy offspring. Ferdinand fully appreciates the spectacle Prospero has created.

MIRANDA (MARIAH GALE) AND FERDINAND (NICK COURT) ARE SURROUNDED BY GODDESSES IN THE 2006 ROYAL SHAKESPEARE COMPANY PRODUCTION.

SHAKESPEARE EXPLAINED: THE TEMPEST

The main event of the spectacle, however, is its disruption. One of the great interpretative questions of the play is why Prospero disrupts the masque. He says, "I had forgot that foul conspiracy / Of the beast Caliban and his confederates / Against my life." But Caliban, Trinculo, and Stephano pose no serious threat to Prospero at this point in the play. One answer to why Prospero is so upset centers on the first part of the sentence: "I had forgot. . . ." This is exactly how Prospero lost his dukedom the first time: he was so involved in "some vanity of [his] Art" that he ignored the conspiracy Antonio had set up against him. Now, twelve years later, when he has Alonso and Antonio where he wants them, Prospero does it again. Although he transfers his anger and frustration onto Caliban, he is really angry with himself.

It is hard to know whether Prospero really expects that Ferdinand and Miranda will be comforted by what he tells them about the masque's lack of substance, which he then extends into a portrait of reality that makes of everyone (spirits, Ferdinand, Miranda, Prospero, the actors who play them, the audience, and all humans) "such stuff / As dreams are made on." The speech is beautiful, and as full of longing as Caliban's cry to dream again. Here the fictive world, the vision shared in the theater, the theater itself, and the world that holds it are all impermanent. In "the great globe," Shakespeare's audience also would have heard the name of Shakespeare's theater, the Globe (where some performances of the play did, in fact, take place). But the stage is also a metaphor for the world. Prospero's vision is totalizing: "all . . . shall dissolve."

Ferdinand and Miranda leave, wishing Prospero peace. Prospero summons Ariel, and we get the full contrast between what Ariel and Caliban represent to Prospero. Ariel "comes with a thought," gratifying Prospero immediately. Caliban represents all that resists his idealizations, including his idealization of himself.

The scene ends with a demonstration of exactly this contrast. Ariel leads Trinculo, Stephano, and Caliban through the mire and seduces them with dress-up clothes. Caliban is disgusted with them, saying "I will have none on't." They end up being chased by spirits in the shape of hunting dogs. This time Prospero gets involved and helps Ariel do his dirty work.

ACT V, SCENE 1

OVERVIEW

Act V begins with Prospero in his magic robes and in full command. It is 6:00 P.M., the time he had predicted that his and Ariel's work would be done. Ariel reports that the king and his followers are imprisoned and immobilized. They are also either out of their minds or mourning those who are out of their minds. Gonzalo in particular weeps, and Ariel tells Prospero that if he saw them now, he would feel sorry for them. At least, Ariel says, he would if he were human.

Even prompted in this way by Ariel, it takes Prospero a minute to talk himself into feeling sympathy. But he reasons that if Ariel, who is not human, can sense their pain, then, as a fellow human, he himself should be moved to pity. Despite his anger, he will choose virtue over vengeance. He will break the spell, restore their senses and their sanity, and let them be themselves again.

Prospero sends Ariel to fetch Alonso and company. Alone onstage, he sums up the power he has wielded in his life as a magician, addressing himself to the spirits of nature he has commanded ("Ye elves of hills, brooks, standing lakes, and groves . . ."). In this speech, he claims powers beyond even what we saw when he caused the tempest at the beginning of the play. He has caused earthquakes and wielded the thunderbolt of Jove. He even claims to have waked the dead.

But then he says that he will give all this up: "But this rough magic / I here abjure." He will use his magic to summon music, but after that, he will break and bury his magic staff and drown his book.

Ariel brings in the charmed—and in some cases, traumatized—members of Alonso's court, and they stand within the magic circle that Prospero has drawn on the ground. Alonso is still in despair, and Sebastian and Antonio still believe they are fighting imaginary demons, just as they had been at the end of Act III. Gonzalo weeps. Prospero addresses them each in turn while they are still "spell-stopped." Now that he actually sees Gonzalo, Prospero weeps "fellowly drops." His address to the unrepentant (and unhearing) Antonio remains deeply divided: he accuses him of being unnatural, even as he says that he forgives him. Then, before they come completely to consciousness, Prospero takes off his magic robes and dresses himself as he used to dress in Milan. Ariel sings merrily as he helps Prospero dress.

Everyone in the magic circle slowly wakes to solemn music. Alonso and Gonzalo are pained and uncertain what to believe, even after Prospero has spoken to them and embraced them. But Alonso gives Prospero back his dukedom and begs his pardon. Prospero says nothing, although his pardon of Alonso is implicit in everything that follows. His treatment of Antonio is the exact opposite. Prospero says he forgives Antonio, but he privately threatens Sebastian and Antonio with disclosing their plot against the king, and his address to Antonio keeps him under tight rein. Antonio has not repented, but he has no choice but to let Prospero take his dukedom back.

Alonso still grieves the loss of his son Ferdinand, and when Prospero says he has lost his own daughter "in this last tempest," Alonso expresses the wish that the two of them were alive and ruling Naples together. As if on cue, Prospero pulls aside a curtain and reveals Ferdinand and Miranda playing (and playfully cheating at) chess. Ferdinand and Alonso are reunited. Miranda is amazed at the new people she sees:

Prospero is less impressed, remarking only that "'Tis new to thee"; but Miranda's admiration is matched by Alonso's wonder at her. He thinks she is a goddess. Ferdinand introduces her, and Alonso gives his consent to

NINETEENTH-CENTURY ARTIST LUCY MADOX BROWN'S OIL PAINTING DEPICTS MIRANDA AND FERDINAND PLAYING CHESS.

the marriage. Gonzalo calls down "a blessed crown" on Ferdinand and Miranda, and joyfully summarizes the happy conclusion to all that has followed on the apparent disaster.

Ariel brings on the ship's crew, including the boatswain, who expresses bewilderment at the survival of everyone. Prospero at last sends Ariel to lead in Trinculo, Stephano, and Caliban. Caliban, like Miranda, is amazed to see the new humans ("these be brave spirits indeed") and to see Prospero dressed as the duke of Milan. Sebastian and Antonio ridicule the drunken Trinculo and Stephano, and Antonio immediately sees Caliban as an opportunity for exploitation. Prospero, for the first time, acknowledges Caliban as his own. Caliban recognizes his mistake in idealizing Stephano, and declares that after this he will be wise "And seek for grace."

Prospero invites Alonso and company to spend the night in his dwellings, promising to tell them his story. His last charge to Ariel is to give them good winds for the trip back to Naples, after which Ariel will be free to the elements at last.

ANALYSIS

At the beginning of Act V, Prospero has all his enemies under his control. Now he has to decide what to do with them: whether to take revenge or forgive them. He opts to forgive, even though—despite what he says—only Alonso is penitent. It has been argued that Prospero made this decision long ago: he will not take revenge because he wants Miranda to marry Ferdinand and become queen of Naples. It could also be argued that he has already caused his enemies some pain. Trinculo, Stephano, and Caliban have had their joints attacked and muscles cramped by Prospero's spirits. Alonso has been wracked by grief, guilt, madness, and suicidal despair. Even the good Gonzalo's optimism has been exhausted by anxiety and confusion. Ariel reminds Prospero of this.

What is new in this scene, rather, may be Prospero's admission of kinship with his fellow humans, and his decision to let them "be themselves." He acknowledges that he, too, feels passions (which we saw in his disruption of the masque). And he acknowledges, however much Ariel has to prompt him to see it, that he is "one of their kind." What follows from this is not just forgiveness (which would leave him still in control), but something that, for Prospero, is even more radical. He will give up control. He will let them be who and what they are.

Prospero's surrender of his magic may be of a piece with this, but ultimately, why Prospero gives up magic remains one of the great, unresolved mysteries of the play. His speech ("Ye elves of hills, brooks, standing lakes, and groves . . .") is adapted from lines spoken by the sorceress Medea in Ovid's *Metamorphoses* (Book 7, 263–289), and Medea's sorcery is a form of black magic—witchcraft—that Shakespeare's contemporaries would have recognized as damnable. This could imply that Prospero's magic has been less virtuous and more like the magic of Sycorax than he has wanted to believe, and some have argued that this is why Prospero must give it up. Others have argued that Prospero doesn't need his magic anymore, or that his magic only works on the island and won't work in Milan. There have been as many readings of Prospero's renunciation of magic as there are interpretations of the play.

But both Prospero and Caliban have changed, however subtly. Prospero continues to describe Caliban in dismissive terms, although there seems to be a kind of grudging admiration for Sycorax in his last description of her. It remains impossible, as always, to tell for certain if "demi-devil" is to be understood literally or figuratively. But what is new in Prospero comes next:

> TWO OF THESE FELLOWS YOU
> MUST KNOW AND OWN; THIS THING OF
> DARKNESS I ACKNOWLEDGE MINE.

This can, of course, be taken at face value: Trinculo and Stephano serve Alonso, and Caliban serves Prospero. (*Own* here means "acknowledge," not "possess.") But for Prospero, who has so often projected his own failings, failures, limitations, and least savory impulses onto Caliban, this may also amount to finally taking responsibility for the parts of himself he has projected onto Caliban. He may also be taking responsibility for his own role in shaping Caliban as he is, even if that means admitting his failures as an educator, surrogate parent, and governor (since he has claimed lordship of the island). But at the symbolic level, "this thing of darkness" implies the many things Prospero has preferred not to see. In this sense, acknowledgment is a major reversal.

Caliban is subtly but significantly different in this scene as well. Caliban has clearly learned from his experience with Stephano and Trinculo. He has outstripped them in discernment, impulse control, and basic dignity, and he has recognized what a fool he was to idealize Stephano. But Caliban is hardly the only character who has idealized a stranger in this play, and it is arguable that Caliban sees Stephano and Trinculo more clearly now than, say, Miranda and Ferdinand see one another. Further, although Caliban has learned his lesson and acknowledges that he acted like an idiot, he does not curse himself, as he did in bitterness at his first appearance in the play. Caliban remains a loose end in the play: Shakespeare does not tell us what will happen to him, and it can be argued that he has no good options. But Caliban has outgrown Trinculo and Stephano, and he shows vastly more range and potential for growth than Antonio. For all the distortion that attaches to him, for all his "disproportion," Caliban resists simplification and caricature to the end.

Ariel is simply free.

EPILOGUE

OVERVIEW

In the epilogue, Prospero steps forward and addresses the audience without his magic. Prospero's power has passed to the audience. We are now in the position that used to be his: he is the prisoner, and we are the ones with the power to confine or release him. Prospero appeals to our recognition that we, too, will need mercy someday. He ends by asking for our indulgence and our "prayer"—which is our applause.

ANALYSIS

Shakespeare scholar Stephen Orgel has argued that this epilogue is unlike any other in Shakespeare, in that Prospero addresses us not as the actor playing Prospero but as the fictional character. But even as a fictional character, Prospero has been a stager of plays. Now, without his magic, Prospero also lacks the ability to impose a spectacle that we must accept as real—as we initially accepted the tempest in the first scene. Here he asks our pardon, and with the word *deceiver*, he reminds us that in the first scene he deceived us, too.

The epilogue completes the set of frames through which we have watched the play (and watched others watching). The tempest of the first scene turned out to be framed by Prospero's art. But now Prospero's art—and Prospero the artist—are framed by us, the living, breathing audience in the theater. We hold the power to sustain or dismiss the fiction, and to ensure or deny the success of the project ("Which was to please"). Without the power of his art, and having let us "be ourselves," Prospero must now rely on our human sympathy. The true power of the theater depends ultimately not on the autocratic artist, but rather on a generous collaboration of artist and audience, who have a common stake in mercy and indulgence. We signal this by our applause.

LIST OF CHARACTERS

Prospero—A powerful magician, and the protagonist of the play. Prospero was the duke of Milan until he was ousted by his younger brother, Antonio. He now lives in exile on the island with his daughter, Miranda.

Miranda—Prospero's daughter, nearly fifteen years old.

Ariel—An airy spirit who performs Prospero's magic.

Caliban—Son of the (deceased) witch Sycorax, formerly part of Prospero's household and now Prospero's slave.

Antonio—The current duke of Milan and Prospero's brother, who usurped Prospero's dukedom twelve years before the start of the play.

Alonso—King of Naples, who helped Antonio oust Prospero in exchange for subjecting the formerly independent Milan to Naples.

Ferdinand—Alonso's son, prince of Naples.

Gonzalo—One of Alonso's councilors, who helped Prospero survive the coup.

Sebastian—Alonso's brother, open to corruption by Antonio.

Trinculo—Alonso's jester, and a clown.

Stephano—Alonso's drunken butler.

Boatswain, Ship's Master, Mariners—Seamen on the ship carrying King Alonso back from North Africa to Italy. The boatswain is competent, realistic, and impatient at the interference of the royal party as he and the mariners try to save the ship.

Adrian and Francisco—Members of Alonso's court.

Juno, Ceres, Iris—Goddesses played by Prospero's spirits in the wedding masque.

Various spirits who serve Prospero.

ANALYSIS OF MAJOR CHARACTERS

PROSPERO

At one time Prospero's studies let him rise above normal human limits but also cost him his dukedom. Twelve years later he is a powerful magician who still loves his books more than his dukedom, but who has the chance to set things right. His strongest motive for getting his dukedom back and leaving the island may be the need to secure the future of his daughter, Miranda, whom he loves. But he also remains angry at his brother and Alonso.

Prospero easily uses his magic to get his enemies under control. More challenging are the things he would prefer to avoid: confessing his past to Miranda; confronting the resistance of Ariel and Caliban; standing back to allow Miranda to grow past him and turn to Ferdinand; and confronting the "darkness" of his own feelings, among them rage and frustration at what he cannot control and what he cannot make perfect, in others and in himself. This is represented, for him, by Caliban.

Through the course of the play, Prospero comes to accept his human limitations and the need to rebuild his connection with other humans. He forgives his enemies, frees them, gives up the magic that has given him such extraordinary power, and frees Ariel. At the end of the play, he acknowledges even Caliban as his own.

Prospero is at the center of the play, and yet also, peculiarly, at its margins, as he engineers a happy ending that, ironically, will cost him the companionship of the two characters he loves most—Ariel and his daughter—and will end with his renunciation of magic. One of the central

PETER FONDA PLAYED PROSPERO
IN A 1998 TELEVISION PRODUCTION
OF THE PLAY.

questions of the play is why Prospero gives up magic. Many have seen a parallel between Prospero's surrender of magic and Shakespeare's retirement from the theater, and when Prospero steps before the audience in the epilogue, stripped of his powers, it is easy to imagine Shakespeare passing on his power as an artist. This does not make Prospero a self-portrait of Shakespeare, however, any more than his relationship with Caliban makes him simply a figure of English imperialism. Shakespeare's powerful, irascible, conflicted magician remains very much his own character.

MIRANDA

Miranda, whose name means "wonder" or "worthy to be admired," is intelligent, compassionate, virtuous, loyal, and beautiful. Nearly fifteen years old, she has been educated by Prospero, loves him, and tries, for the most part, to do exactly as he wants. But she has not surrendered her independent judgment completely. She suspects immediately that Prospero has caused the storm and says that she would have done things differently had she "been any god of power." When she thinks that Prospero is telling her not to feel compassion for the suffering she has witnessed, she refuses to follow his advice. This tells us what she believes her father capable of and shows that she already follows her own moral compass. In other ways as well, she is stronger and less naïve than she is sometimes taken to be. She reacts to Caliban with understandable aversion since his attempt to rape her, but after he boasts that he would have populated the island with Calibans if he had been successful, she rebukes him in a speech that shocked some editors so much that they assigned it to Prospero instead ("Abhorred slave, / Which any print of goodness wilt not take . . ."). It is true that she sounds a lot like her father in this speech. But her anger is independently justified.

In the few hours of the play, Miranda's life changes enormously. She learns the story of her life and meets other humans for the first time. She falls in love with Ferdinand and goes against her father's orders not to speak to him. She is candid about her feelings in speaking with Ferdinand, and she proposes marriage with a boldness that recalls Shakespeare's Juliet. Much is made of Miranda's innocence, but she is strong in her innocence and undaunted. This extends to her enthusiasm for the "brave new world." She lacks experience, but she also teases Ferdinand when he cheats at chess, and we have the impression that she will mature quickly and gracefully in the company of other humans.

ARIEL

Unlike Caliban, Ariel is not human. Ariel is a spirit of the natural elements, associated with air but at home in all four, and able to take on different shapes and travel from location to location in the blink of an eye. It is generally accepted that he—or she—has no certain sex or gender: Ariel is referred to once as "he," but nearly always takes on female roles (nymphs, Harpy, Ceres); and since females were played by boys on the Elizabethan stage, Ariel could easily have been read as androgynous. Ariel does

A PENSIVE ARIEL (CYNTHIA SIEDEN) PERFORMED IN A 2007 PRODUCTION AT THE ROYAL OPERA HOUSE, LONDON.

Prospero's bidding but wants, above all, to be free. To get this freedom, Ariel is obligingly cheerful and affectionate. Ariel delights us, too, and is often understood as standing for the poetic imagination, or the collaboration of the natural elements and the mind of the artist to make music, poetry, and art. Ariel is also observant enough to be able to say how s/he would react, "were I human," and it is Ariel who takes Prospero the last steps toward recognizing his own humanity. But Ariel is finally of a different order, joyfully anticipating being free to the elements once more.

CALIBAN

Caliban is the son of the witch Sycorax, who was exiled to the island when she was pregnant with him. We do not know how old Caliban was when Sycorax died, but he was at least twelve when Prospero arrived on the island. This makes him at least twenty-four when the play begins. We do not know who his father was: Prospero calls him "a born devil" and a "poisonous slave, got by the devil himself," but the play never confirms if this is literal or figurative. The play does confirm that Caliban is strange looking and probably deformed in some way. But Caliban is human, or at least half human (if we accept that his father was the devil). Whatever disproportion he embodies attaches to "one of our kind."

Caliban loves the island and knows its features intimately. When Prospero first landed, Caliban shared the secrets of survival with him. Caliban was educated by Prospero and Miranda, and was part of their household until his attempt to rape Miranda. He claims the island as his inheritance from Sycorax and views Prospero as a usurper, but we do not know if he asserted this claim before Prospero enslaved him.

Caliban is irreducibly complicated. He is often associated with the natural world and with the baser, more animalistic side of human nature, but this ignores how much he is also the product of twelve years of Prospero's culture. He has the greatest range of language of any character in the play:

I'LL BE WISE HEREAFTER, AND SEEK FOR GRACE.

its harshest, its most lyrical, its most direct, its most artificial, its most reckless, and its most richly descriptive. He parallels Antonio in staging a coup against Prospero, and is both brutally pragmatic and childishly graphic in his murderous designs. Yet he is less corrupt than Antonio. He is naïve to the point of foolishness in his adoration of Stephano, but, importantly, he learns from his experience. In this sense, he is the empiricist of the play. He is wistful, bitter, joyful, resentful, ingratiating, aggressive, longing, and sometimes murderous. He knows and loves the island, its rocks and wildlife no less than its music. He resists simple definition as tenaciously as he resists Prospero.

A CLOSER LOOK

- THEMES

- MOTIFS

- SYMBOLS

- LANGUAGE

- INTERPRETING THE PLAY

Paramount's 1958 ▶
production, *Tempest* (*La
Tempesta*), paired Geoffrey
Horne and Silvana Mangano.

TEMPEST

NT PRESENTS
RENTIIS PRODUCTION

N HEFLIN
NA MANGANO
CA LINDFORS
FFREY HORNE

OSCAR HOMOLKA
HELMUT DANTINE
AGNES MOOREHEAD
ROBERT KEITH
and VITTORIO GASSMAN

PRODUCED BY
NO DeLAURENTIIS

Directed by ALBERTO LATTUADA
creenplay by LOUIS PETERSON
AND ALBERTO LATTUADA
ased on a novel by Alexander Pushkin

TECHNICOLOR
FILMED IN
TECHNIRAMA

66929
66929

Chapter
One

CHAPTER THREE

a Closer Look

THEMES

THE POWER OF ART

In *The Tempest*, art and the artist are credited with extraordinary power. The play then investigates the scope, the use, and, finally, the limits of that power.

The Tempest begins with a spectacular demonstration of the power of Prospero's art: just after we have seen the storm overpower the ship in what appears to be a display of nature's power over human beings, we learn that it has all been staged and controlled by Prospero's magic. More spectacles follow, and Prospero's art is specifically related to the power of theater. But art is also a means of securing and maintaining political power. Music, for instance, has the power to calm the waves and soothe the passions, but it is also a metaphor for Antonio's power to "set all hearts i'th'state / To what tune pleased his ear." Prospero's magic, which is also his technology, serves as a means of surveillance and control, sometimes by illusion, sometimes by seduction, and sometimes by physical coercion. Technological superiority, as Caliban notes ruefully, translates into superior force: "I must obey. His art is of such power, / It would control my dam's god Setebos / And make a vassal of him."

Yet the play also explores the limits of that force. First, not all of Prospero's "present fancies" can be "enacted," not even by the spirits he has called from their confines. Prospero cannot force Antonio to have a conscience or to regret usurping his dukedom. Prospero cannot force Caliban to take whatever ideal shape—physical or moral—Prospero might want. Second, Prospero can control what people see and experience, and he can shut them down ("They cannot budge till your release"). But this also isolates him, and them, from interaction both with other humans and with the surrounding world. In the end Prospero opts to "restore their senses"—to give them back the ability to experience the world—and to let them "be themselves." This is his most important ethical decision in the play.

At the end of *The Tempest*, Prospero gives up his "so potent art," and in the epilogue, he presents himself to us without it: "Now my charms are all o'erthrown, / And what strength I have's mine own, / Which is most faint."

O BRAVE NEW WORLD, THAT HAS SUCH PEOPLE IN'T!

Power passes to the audience. Even the most potent artist's power to create a world depends, finally, on the audience's ratification, indulgence, and applause.

THE TRUE NATURE OF BONDAGE AND FREEDOM

The Tempest is full of instances of bondage, slavery, servitude, and confinement. Ariel was confined by Sycorax in a pine until "freed" by Prospero, but Prospero keeps Ariel in service partly by threats of re-imprisoning Ariel in an oak. Caliban has been enslaved, and physically confined, since his attempted rape of Miranda. Ferdinand is imprisoned and put to forced labor, and all of Prospero's enemies are finally "prisoners," "confined together." All depend on Prospero for their release.

If the idea of "release" from bondage seems simple enough, however, the same thing cannot be said for freedom. The play offers multiple images of freedom. The liberty sought by Ariel is a pure and total freedom: we imagine Ariel freed "to the elements," "as free / As mountain winds." Ariel's freedom is absolute. But Ariel is not human.

The play also contains images of false freedom: the "freedom" Caliban chooses when he subjects himself to Stephano, or that Antonio chose when he traded the independence of Milan to become duke. Antonio plots now to recover some of that freedom by murdering Alonso and making Sebastian king: "Draw thy sword—one stroke / Shall free thee from the tribute which thou payest, / And I the King shall love thee." But this is largely what Caliban does with Stephano: there is little pretense that Antonio is free of anything but conscience.

Between the absolute freedom of Ariel and the false freedom of Antonio (and Caliban, until he is free of his illusions about Stephano), the play offers us a third option—namely, bonds that are freely chosen. Ferdinand's service for Miranda—for which he gladly sacrifices "liberty"—is straight from the conventions of courtly love, but here, the metaphors are vested with fresh meaning. Ferdinand pledges himself to Miranda "with a heart as willing / As bondage e'er of freedom," and they exchange hands. Such bonds, freely chosen and willingly maintained, may represent the highest freedom in the play.

The characters whose freedom is most in question at the end of the play are Caliban and Prospero. Caliban is freed from his illusions about Stephano, and he tells Prospero he'll "be wise hereafter, / And seek for grace," but Caliban is more persuasive as a figure of resistance than as a figure of freedom. We do not know if Caliban will go to Naples or remain on the island, and if he stays on the island, whether that will represent freedom or a terrible isolation. Equally ambiguous is Prospero's status at the end of the play. He has made a free, ethical choice to release the others, and he has given them the freedom to "be themselves." But in the end, Prospero's freedom depends on forgiveness, which he seeks from us. The play ends with his request that we set him free.

THE SUBTLETY OF TRANSFORMATION

In his narrative about how he lost his dukedom, Prospero claims that Antonio "new created / The creatures that were mine, I say: or changed 'em, / Or else new formed 'em." But it turns out that this is something that Prospero's art cannot do. The great transformations that take place in the play happen in the spaces where Prospero relinquishes control: he sets up the conditions that lead to Alonso's grief and remorse, or that lead to Ferdinand and Miranda's falling in love, but in the end, these transformations take their own course. At its most powerful, Prospero's art collaborates with spirits he has harnessed from nature, and Ariel embodies nature and the natural elements in their ever-changing forms as they are "correspondent to [the] command" of Prospero's design. Ariel's song "Full fathom five ..." presents what may be Prospero's own vision of a transformation in which "Nothing ...

doth fade, / But doth suffer a sea-change / Into something rich and strange."
But when Prospero has his crisis in Act IV and destroys the "vanity of [his]
Art," he substitutes a vision in which everything on Earth "dissolves" like his
"insubstantial pageant faded." The play does not decide between these two
opposing visions. But when Prospero lifts the spell from Alonso and Gonzalo
in Act V, and "dissolves" the charm that held them captive, he describes
their returning consciousness in metaphors that evoke transformation and
regeneration in the natural world: morning melts the darkness, and their
understanding returns like "the approaching tide."

MOTIFS

WONDERS AND MONSTERS

The Tempest is full of encounters with strange creatures, as well as natural
creatures mistaken for wonders. Miranda ("O you wonder!") first mistakes
Ferdinand for a spirit, and Ferdinand mistakes her for a goddess: "Most
sure, the goddess / On whom these airs attend." His father Alonso does the
same thing in Act V: "Is she the goddess that hath severed us / And brought
us thus together?" This mistake is repeated in the register of comedy when
Caliban mistakes Stephano for "a brave god." Caliban learns his mistake;
but at the end of the play, Miranda still idealizes the humans she sees: "O
wonder! / . . . O brave new world / That has such people in't."

The treatment of monsters is more complex. Caliban is repeatedly called
a monster by Trinculo and Stephano, but although Caliban is deformed
in some way, Trinculo himself confirms that Caliban is human: "this is no
fish, but an islander. . . ." The literal monsters in the play are the Harpy
and the strange shapes that bring out the banquet in Act III: "Who, though
they are of monstrous shape, yet note / Their manners are more gentle,
kind, than of / Our human generation you shall find / Many—nay, almost
any." Prospero underlines this observation by Gonzalo, adding that "some

of you there present / Are worse than devils." These two threads come together at the end of Act III when Alonso recognizes his crime in having deposed Prospero and sent him and Miranda out to die: "O it is monstrous, monstrous!" Being morally "monstrous" or "unnatural" (as Prospero later calls Antonio) is worse than being physically misshapen.

DREAMS AND DROWSINESS

Dreams and drowsiness serve as key metaphors for the sense of unreality that many of the characters experience on the island, as well as for the elusiveness of what we most desire. Miranda's memories of her early childhood are "rather like a dream than an assurance / That my remembrance warrants." Ferdinand notes that "My spirits, as in a dream, are all bound up." Drowsiness is both the occasion and a metaphor for Antonio to seduce Sebastian into a conspiracy to kill the king: "surely / It is a sleepy language, and thou speak'st / Out of thy sleep." The two great dream speeches are those of Caliban (". . . I cried to dream again.") and Prospero (". . . We are such stuff / As dreams are made on. . . ."). Both speeches are occasioned by the desire to give comfort; both conjure visions of clouds, whether bearing riches or amazing cities; both evoke the longing for what we can neither grasp nor make permanent. Prospero says that the dreamers are as ephemeral as their dreams.

THE ISLAND

The island is both a literal and a symbolic site in the play. According to the basic plot, the island is located in the Mediterranean Sea somewhere between Naples, Italy, and Tunis in North Africa. Caliban can describe its physical features, natural resources, and wildlife in detail.

But the island also has symbolic functions in the play. It is the place of illusion, governed by Prospero's magic. Prospero cites the "subtleties o'th'isle that will not let you / Believe things certain."

The island is a place of projections, and different characters see it differently. To Gonzalo, the island is lush and green. To Antonio and Sebastian, the island is barren and brown. These conflicting views are not reconciled.

According to a network of allusions, the island stands for the New World. The play names Bermuda ("the still-vexed Bermoothes"), and implicit New World references evoke territories as far-flung as Patagonia, Brazil, Virginia, and Maine.

Finally, the island is a symbol for the stage. Shakespeare makes this explicit in the epilogue, when Prospero asks the audience to release him from "this bare island." But the analogy works throughout the play: the stage is a site of magic, illusion, projection, and power.

MAGIC

Magic is usually referred to as Prospero's art, and it often stands for all the human arts. Most specifically, magic is a symbol for the theater. Prospero's magic works by many of the same means as theater, and, reciprocally, the metaphor calls attention to the "magic" of theater and its power to enchant.

But Prospero's magic is also a technology. It is the means by which he controls the storm, and it is his means of surveillance and control of the other humans on the island. We tend to think of art and technology

WHAT SEEST THOU ELSE IN THE DARK BACKWARD AND ABYSM OF TIME?

as opposites, but originally they are the same thing: the Latin word *ars* and the Greek word *techne* both mean "art." Prospero says he excelled at the liberal arts, which include rhetoric, grammar, logic, mathematics, geometry, astronomy, and music. But the Renaissance also recognized arts of statesmanship, arts of courtly behavior, arts of reckoning (mathematics and navigation), and many more. The play's investigation of the power and limits of art thus extends, potentially, to all the human arts, sciences, and technology.

ARIEL AND CALIBAN AS SYMBOLS

Ariel and Caliban are characters who can never be reduced to symbols alone. But they also, frequently, carry symbolic meaning, especially as a pair. Ariel is associated with air, and Caliban with the earth. Ariel represents the freedom of the mind, thought, and the imagination. Caliban represents the limitations of the body, the passions, the beast in man. Ariel represents soaring spirit, Caliban the weight of matter. Ariel stands for all that comes easily to Prospero's art; Caliban represents all that resists Prospero's art. In this way Ariel and Caliban also stand for parts of Prospero himself, and Caliban, especially, becomes a symbol of what Prospero is loathe to recognize, or cannot control, not least in himself. These symbols are not absolute in the play, however. For instance, although we associate Ariel with air, Ariel inhabits all four elements and is joyously comfortable in the natural world. Ariel, no less than Caliban, is a symbol of nature, even though they represent different sides of nature.

LANGUAGE

The Tempest both uses language and is about language. Characters repeatedly express surprise when they hear their own language—Italian, but spoken, of course, in English—spoken by strangers on the island. "My language? Heavens!" (Ferdinand, Act I, Scene 2.) "Where the devil should he learn our language?" (Stephano, Act II, Scene 2.) Prospero and Miranda regard their language as a gift they bestow on Caliban, and Caliban's retort has become the quintessential expression of rage and near despair at the contradictions entailed in the dubious gift of "the master's language": "You taught me language; and my profit on't / Is, I know how to curse." By contrast, sung and spoken language come to share music's ability to comfort, to soothe, and to bless. The following discussion traces the arc from language used almost as pure sound, in Ariel's songs, to language used strategically as an instrument of expression and sometimes contest, still sounded, in the speeches of Prospero and Caliban.

The musical qualities of language as pure sound are used for both harmony and resistance in the play. Ariel sings and plays songs that use actual music and drums, but the verse also turns the rhythms and sounds of the language itself into music:

> COME UNTO THESE YELLOW SANDS,
> AND THEN TAKE HANDS.
> CURTSIED WHEN YOU HAVE, AND KISSED
> THE WILD WAVES WHIST;
> FOOT IT FEATLY HERE AND THERE,
> AND SWEET SPRITES BEAR
> THE BURDEN . . .

Alliterations (curtsied . . . kissed) join spondees (consecutive stressed syllables) in the "wild waves whist": the sounds themselves join hands and dance. The device of combining alliteration and rhythm is repeated in the couplet—"foot it featly"; "sweet sprites bear"—and the energy spills over into the next line with both enjambment and more alliteration: "sweet sprites bear / The burden").

The use of the physical properties of sound to celebrate resistance to an imposed order, on the other hand, is clearest in Caliban's "freedom song":

> 'BAN, 'BAN, CACALIBAN
> HAS A NEW MASTER: GET A NEW MAN.

At this moment in the play, Caliban has more freedom in his song than in his situation, since he has escaped Prospero only to subject himself to Stephano.

In addition to repetitions of sounds (alliteration, assonance, rhyme), Shakespeare uses many other figures of repetition and arrangement throughout the play. Shakespeare uses conspicuous figures and distortions of language in Prospero's speeches to signal his state of mind. When Prospero is conflicted, either because he doesn't want to have to admit something or when his feelings are at odds with what he thinks he must say, his language becomes marked by interruptions, digressions, and disturbances of word order. This is especially true when he tells Miranda the story of his life in the second scene of the play.

On the other hand, when Prospero speaks from strong passions without trying to correct them, he has a marked tendency to hyperbole and figures of repetition. The most complete case of repetition and hyperbole communicating emotional distress is his lament about how ineffectual his efforts at shaping Caliban have been:

> A DEVIL, A BORN DEVIL, ON WHOSE NATURE
> NURTURE CAN NEVER STICK; ON WHOM MY PAINS,
> HUMANELY TAKEN ALL, ALL LOST, QUITE LOST!

This is as highly worked a passage as Ariel's songs, and as packed with rhetorical figures. Prospero repeats the word *devil* with amplification. The repetition of similar-sounding words with different meanings in "nature/Nurture" has the same effect as Ariel's songs: the sound similarity makes the meaning seem inevitably true, whether or not it is an accurate description of Caliban. The sheer overload of alliteration and assonance (*nature/nurture . . . never*; "pains humanely taken") emphasizes Prospero's frustration at repeated efforts that have not had the effect he wanted, and the hyperbole ("never") is amplified with repetition and assonance in "all, all lost, quite lost!"

If Prospero's language shows the most contortion in the play, the most versatile speaker in the play is Caliban. So far we have seen repetition and sound play in the language of a single speaker. But a good instance of repetition and sound play being marshaled in a contest for meaning comes in the first interchange between Prospero and Caliban. When Prospero first calls Caliban, he insults him (calling him "slave," "earth," "tortoise"); and when Caliban doesn't come fast enough, Prospero adds an insult to Caliban's mother:

> PROSPERO: Thou poisonous slave, got by the devil himself / Upon
> thy wicked dam; come forth!

Caliban answers by taking up Prospero's own words:

> CALIBAN: As wicked dew as ere my mother brushed / With
> raven's feather from unwholesome fen / Drop on you both.

By turning "wicked dam" to "wicked dew," Caliban not only turns Prospero's insult into a curse against him, but also rejects and effectively rewrites Prospero's version of reality. First, far from being wicked herself, Sycorax is depicted here as *purging* the unwholesome fens of their poisons. The dew is wicked, not Sycorax. Second, Caliban reminds Prospero that he and Sycorax had a life on the island—made habitable by Sycorax—before the arrival of Prospero. This supports his claim to the island, which he will make a few lines later. Third, it calls attention to the fact that Prospero himself uses dew in his magic (which is why he sent Ariel to "the still-vexed Bermoothes"). Caliban can be throwing the similarity between Prospero and Sycorax back in Prospero's face. This is the strategy of a formidable opponent, but it is not the language of someone on whose nature nurture has never stuck at all. If anything, Prospero may regret how well Caliban has learned from his example.

Shakespeare has in many ways made Caliban the linguist of the play. His curses, as just cited, are indeed harsh, and we have noted his celebratory "'Ban, 'Ban, Cacaliban." But he speaks an astonishing range of languages. In his subservience to Stephano he mimics courtly speech to the point of parody: "Wilt thou be pleas'd to hearken once again to the suit I made to thee?" He is capable of language of surpassing lyrical beauty:

> BE NOT AFEARD. THE ISLE IS FULL OF NOISES,
> SOUNDS AND SWEET AIRS THAT GIVE DELIGHT AND HURT NOT.
> SOMETIMES A THOUSAND TWANGLING INSTRUMENTS
> WILL HUM ABOUT MINE EARS; AND SOMETIMES VOICES,
> THAT IF I THEN HAD WAKED AFTER LONG SLEEP,
> WILL MAKE ME SLEEP AGAIN; AND THEN IN DREAMING,
> THE CLOUDS, METHOUGHT, WOULD OPEN AND SHOW RICHES
> READY TO DROP UPON ME, THAT WHEN I WAKED
> I CRIED TO DREAM AGAIN.

So much contributes to this speech and its poignancy, but its effects of sound, too, show all the artfulness we see in speeches to which Shakespeare devoted special care. The sound repetitions are sparer and farther apart ("isle ... delight," "noises ... voices"), and the sense of longing is reinforced by longer intervals between the repetitions ("sometimes ... sometimes"). But the key device is "the slow return" of the long series: "waked ... sleep ... sleep again; ... dreaming ... waked ... dream again." We experience this as "artless," as pure longing. But Shakespeare knew his figures well, and Puttenham, whose *Arte of English Poesie* (1589) Shakespeare used throughout his career, would have recognized the powerful effect of the repetitions, both for the ear and for the mind.

Even Caliban's ordinary language is fluent, whether expansive and

'BAN,' BAN, CACALIBAN HAS A NEW MASTER: GET A NEW MAN.

inventive or pointedly direct. Frustrated that Trinculo and Stephano are seduced by the "trumpery"—the fancy dress-up clothes that Ariel hangs up to distract them—he cries, "Let it alone, thou fool; it is but trash." But earlier, in describing the island, he says,

> I PRITHEE, LET ME BRING THEE WHERE CRABS GROW;
> AND I WITH MY LONG NAILS WILL DIG THEE PIG-NUTS;
> SHOW THEE A JAY'S NEST, AND INSTRUCT THEE HOW
> TO SNARE THE NIMBLE MARMOSET; I'LL BRING THEE
> TO CLUSTERING FILBERTS, AND SOMETIMES I'LL GET THEE
> YOUNG SCAMELS FROM THE ROCK.

Stephen Greenblatt, a Shakespeare scholar, has praised the "rich, irreducible concreteness" of this verse, which "compels us to acknowledge the independence and integrity of Caliban's construction of reality." But it also has the same temporality of "sometimes" as did "sometimes a thousand twangling instruments" and "sometimes voices"; only this time, what Caliban describes is in his control: "and sometimes I'll get thee / Young scamels from the rock." This is Caliban in his own time, and with an openness to experience far removed from the defensive battles of "wicked dam" versus "wicked dew." In both cases, however, Shakespeare shows us Caliban as a fluent, adept, versatile, and inventive speaker of the language the native Europeans claim for their own.

TRANSFORMATION THROUGH LANGUAGE

Shakespeare uses the possible coincidences—or oppositions—of sound and sense to a variety of effects in the play. In Ariel's best-known song, the beauty of the sounds almost makes us forget that what is being described is the transformation of a corpse:

> FULL FATHOM FIVE THY FATHER LIES,
> OF HIS BONES ARE CORAL MADE;
> THOSE ARE PEARLS THAT WERE HIS EYES,
> NOTHING OF HIM THAT DOTH FADE
> BUT DOTH SUFFER A SEA-CHANGE
> INTO SOMETHING RICH AND STRANGE.

Once again Shakespeare uses alliteration (full fathom five . . . father; suffer . . . sea . . . something . . . strange), interwoven with assonance (five . . . lies; bones . . . coral; nothing . . . doth; doth suffer . . . something). By the time the last link in this chain of assonance and alliteration comes, reinforced with the end rhyme (suffer . . . sea-change/ . . . something . . . strange), a kind of sensory inevitability already underlies the meaning. We believe that nothing fades, even as the eyes are turned to pearls. The medium of transformation is as much language as the sea, of course; but the modulations of the sound are as palpable to the senses as the sea. It takes a conscious effort to challenge the meaning of the song, or even to remember that what the song tells Ferdinand is, strictly speaking, untrue: his father, Alonso, has not drowned.

INTERPRETING THE PLAY

READING BY DESIGN: THE SYMMETRICAL STRUCTURE OF *THE TEMPEST*

The nine scenes of *The Tempest* are arranged symmetrically. In their edition of *The Tempest*, Virginia Mason Vaughan and Alden Vaughan describe the pattern from the outside in: The first and ninth scenes contain the destruction and restoration of the ship. The second and eighth scenes are concerned with Prospero, Miranda, and Ferdinand. The third and seventh are concerned with Alonso, Gonzalo, Sebastian, and Antonio. The fourth and sixth are concerned with Caliban, Trinculo, and Stephano. And the fifth and central scene "showcases Ferdinand and Miranda's betrothal." Mark Rose, who first demonstrated this pattern in his book *Shakespearean Design* (1972), sees the design as a "centerpiece" surrounded by "an extraordinary triple frame composed of distinct character groups."

If we follow this pattern of character groupings further, however, we find an even more thorough symmetry. The very long second scene of the play (Act I, Scene 2) consists of four, very separate, subscenes or encounters. All involve conversations with Prospero, but they are kept quite separate and distinct. (Miranda is actually put to sleep during Prospero's conversation with Ariel.)

In the first encounter of Act I, Scene 2, Prospero removes his magic robes and tells Miranda the story of their lives in Milan before they came to the island. In the second, Prospero meets with Ariel. In the third, Prospero and Miranda confront Caliban. And in the fourth, Prospero and Miranda meet Ferdinand. These encounters are then repeated in reverse order at the end of the play. Prospero shows Miranda and Ferdinand the masque in Act IV.

But at the end of Act IV, Prospero again confronts Caliban. He then meets with Ariel. And after swearing off magic, he gathers into his magic circle the (still unconscious) figures from his past in Milan and removes his magic robes. The rest of Act V, after Alonso and company regain consciousness, corresponds only very loosely to the first scene of the play: the boatswain returns and confirms that the ship is safe, rigged, and ready. But in the rest of the play, the basic pattern holds tightly and clearly.

Shakespeare has taken care that we notice these symmetries, even as we watch the play on stage. Prospero appears in the corresponding scenes—Act I, Scene 2, and Act V, Scene 1—in his full magic robes and then takes them off, in both scenes, when he confronts his past in Milan. This invites interpretation. For instance, Prospero's whole life has been shaped by the contradictory demands—and value systems—of being a duke and being a Neoplatonist mage, and this contradiction is displayed before our eyes in the form of the magic robes and discussions of Milan. What happens on the island then takes place between the "bookends" of these two reckonings with his two roles. It is no accident that in the second of these, Prospero gives up magic and then puts on his Milanese clothing.

Or, to take another example, Prospero and Ariel make contact many times throughout the play, but the pattern of corresponding scenes singles out two in particular for our attention: Act I, Scene 2, and Act V, Scene 1. In these two scenes, Prospero and Ariel also report on the exact time of day (2:00 P.M. and then 6:00 P.M.). The obvious gesture of telling time signals the correspondence of the two scenes for an audience in such an unmistakable way that, again, we are invited to interpret. If we go back and compare the scenes, one of the things we find is that, in some ways, Prospero and Ariel have reversed roles. In Act I, Scene 2, Prospero treats Ariel like a bad student flunking a quiz on Sycorax. In Act V, Scene 1, however, the roles are reversed. Ariel now teaches

Prospero—very gently—to recognize that he is human and that he can feel compassion. Prospero's comment "Dost thou think so, spirit?" is a world apart from where he started.

The most obvious effect of the symmetrical pattern is to focus our attention on Act III, Scene 1, the betrothal of Ferdinand and Miranda, as the heart of the play. This is interesting in itself. The language of the two lovers seems so conventional, and their readiness to fall in love such a given, that it is easy to take this scene for granted. But it is central to the plot: the marriage of Ferdinand and Miranda will unite Milan and Naples, and their offspring—not Antonio or Sebastian—will inherit both.

Making this scene central also puts love at the heart of the play: the love of Ferdinand and Miranda, and also, perhaps, the love of Prospero for Miranda. The betrothal of Ferdinand and Miranda is the play's model of a relationship freely chosen. Miranda and Ferdinand show us liberty in service and freedom in commitment. What they make together—their love, and the potential their union brings for healing and for new life—far surpasses anything that Prospero's art can "enforce." One of the things that is most interesting in this scene is that Prospero stays silent, on the margins. He recognizes that he must allow their affections to take their own course. And he is grateful that they are falling in love, because that is something that he can't, finally, control. Ultimately "they are both in either's powers," not in his. And he blesses "that which breeds between 'em."

The symmetry of scenes thus focuses our attention where we might not have looked before, helps us discover hidden connections and transformations, and offers us new points at which to begin to interpret the play.

WE ARE SUCH STUFF AS DREAMS ARE MADE ON.

SHAKESPEARE EXPLAINED: THE TEMPEST

UNLEASHING FURY: ALLEGORY IN THE TEMPEST

Among the diverse genres Shakespeare puts to use in *The Tempest* are two genres of dramatic allegory. The first is the court masque, in which a whole pageant is a representation of cosmic and social order. Within the masque, the actors represent abstract ideas, sometimes named as such (e.g., "Heroic Virtue" or "Fame"), and sometimes in the guise of a god or goddess. Thus, in Prospero's masque in Act IV of *The Tempest*, Iris, who is also a personified rainbow, represents temperance and the calm after the storm.

The second form of theatrical allegory that Shakespeare puts to use in *The Tempest* is the allegory of the medieval morality plays. In the morality plays—still performed during the Renaissance—actors play parts of the soul, or the seven deadly sins, or a character's "Good Angel" and "Bad Angel," as they battle for the soul of the central character—often an "Everyman." This form of allegory is called *psychomachia* ("battle of the soul"—or, to use our more modern terminology, "battle of the psyche"). Once again the actors play personified abstractions, only this time, their contest represents the inner struggle of the central character.

Shakespeare makes use of the morality tradition in *The Tempest* by having Ariel and Caliban represent dimensions of Prospero's inner self. As part of Prospero, Ariel represents the free life of the mind, and all that aspires to the higher realms of spirit. Caliban, on the other hand, represents the unruly passions, all that resists perfection in Prospero and drags him down, including his temper. This is reinforced by associations that are built up throughout the play. From the beginning, Ariel has been associated with air, and Caliban with the earth. By Act IV, however, Shakespeare encourages us also to see these qualities as parts of Prospero himself. When Prospero says to Ariel, "Spirit, we must prepare to meet with Caliban," he is speaking in the language of psychomachia. He is rallying his free, reasonable side to confront the beast within. Prospero's conversation with Ariel at the beginning of Act V has equally clear echoes of the morality tradition. It is Ariel, his "Good Angel," who urges Prospero to choose virtue over vengeance.

Where Shakespeare leaves the morality play behind is in the fact that Ariel and Caliban are never solely representations of Prospero's inner state. They are independent characters to whom Prospero has ethical obligations, and they both make demands on Prospero for acknowledgment and reciprocity quite apart from how he thinks about them in his head. Prospero has a contract with Ariel. Prospero landed on an island that was already occupied by Caliban. They butt heads as two independent characters.

Shakespeare puts all this to work in the fourth act of the play. First, Prospero stages his idealized court masque. All goes well until Prospero remembers Caliban and disrupts the performance. This moment can itself be read allegorically: Prospero interrupts the most idealistic display of his art when he remembers Caliban, who stands for everything that resists his idealizations. The memory of Caliban's conspiracy also reminds Prospero that he has just repeated what he did twelve years earlier when he lost his dukedom: he has gotten caught up in the "vanity of [his] art" yet again and has forgotten his other tasks.

Regardless of how we interpret the interruption, however, Shakespeare shows us the consequences in a very simple, but very effective, use of both of the kinds of allegory we have identified. First, the "anti-masquers" come on—Caliban, Trinculo and Stephano, stinking of "horse-piss" from the swamp they've been in, dressed up in fancy costumes, and looking (and smelling) like a demented parody of the masque that just ended. So far this is a simple inversion of the proper order of a court masque: the disorder of the anti-masque is supposed to come before the masque, not after. But Shakespeare takes this a step further: the anti-masquers are routed not by the orderly masque but by an angry Prospero eager to "plague them all, / Even to roaring." Act IV ends with a stunningly simple bit of allegory: Prospero "unleashes his fury." For the first and only time in the play, Prospero joins Ariel in doing his dirty work and sets his spirits on Caliban, Trinculo, and Stephano in the form of hunting dogs and hounds. Two of the dogs get their names from Shakespeare's sources; the other two Shakespeare has named himself: "Fury, Fury! There, Tyrant, there! Hark, hark!" Prospero routs the anti-masquers with a display of temper and violence. He may be joining with Ariel to set the dogs on the real Caliban, but the Caliban within him has taken over.

Prospero speaks the language of the morality plays at least two more times in Act V. In his opening conversation with Ariel, he says, "Though with their high wrongs I am struck to th'quick, / Yet with my nobler reason 'gainst my fury / Do I take part." This is clean, classic psychomachia: reason is battling against fury, and Prospero opts to side with reason. The allegory is all in the language here, but in the previous act, we saw his fury unleashed and barking. We know what it can do.

The second, more complex, and more familiarly "Shakespearean" instance comes when Prospero, at the end of the play, says of Caliban, "this thing of darkness I / Acknowledge mine." The line resonates in many ways, but the morality play has taught us to see that on one level, at least, Prospero is speaking of a darkness in himself. Ironically, by acknowledging his allegorical darkness, he may also be able to free Caliban, finally, of his projections and let Caliban be himself. In the end Prospero's allegory must find its way from morality to ethics, and to an acceptance of what is real.

Chronology

1564 William Shakespeare is born on April 23 in Stratford-upon-Avon, England

1578–1582 Span of Shakespeare's "Lost Years," covering the time between leaving school and marrying Anne Hathaway of Stratford

1582 At age eighteen Shakespeare marries Anne Hathaway, age twenty-six, on November 28

1583 Susanna Shakespeare, William and Anne's first child, is born in May, six months after the wedding

1584 Birth of twins Hamnet and Judith Shakespeare

1585–1592 Shakespeare leaves his family in Stratford to become an actor and playwright in a London theater company

1587 Public beheading of Mary, Queen of Scots

1593–1594 The Bubonic (Black) Plague closes theaters in London

1594–1596 As a leading playwright, Shakespeare creates some of his most popular work, including *A Midsummer Night's Dream* and *Romeo and Juliet*

1596 Hamnet Shakespeare dies in August at age eleven, possibly of plague

1596–1597	*The Merchant of Venice* and *Henry IV, Part One*, most likely are written
1599	The Globe Theater opens
1600	*Julius Caesar* is first performed at the Globe
1600–1601	*Hamlet* is believed to have been written
1601–1602	*Twelfth Night* is probably composed
1603	Queen Elizabeth dies; Scottish king James VI succeeds her and becomes England's James I
1604	Shakespeare pens *Othello*
1605	*Macbeth* is composed
1608–1610	London's theaters are forced to close when the plague returns and kills an estimated 33,000 people
1611	*The Tempest* is written
1613	The Globe Theater is destroyed by fire
1614	Reopening of the Globe
1616	Shakespeare dies on April 23
1623	Anne Hathaway, Shakespeare's widow, dies; a collection of Shakespeare's plays, known as the First Folio, is published

Source Notes

p. 39, par. 3, On the masque in *The Tempest* in relation to Shakespeare's audiences, see David Bevington, "*The Tempest* and the Jacobean Court Masque," in *The Politics of the Stuart Court Masque*, ed. David Bevington and Peter Holbrook (Cambridge: Cambridge University Press, 1998), 231.

p. 40, par. 2, For a good overview of Shakespeare's sources, see Virgina Mason Vaughan, and Alden T. Vaughan, Introduction to *The Tempest, by William Shakespeare*, Arden Shakespeare, 3rd series (Walton-on-Thames: Thomas Nelson and Sons, Ltd., 1999). The scenarios from Italian popular theater (*commedia dell'arte*) relevant to *The Tempest* can be found in K. M. Lea, *Italian Popular Comedy* (New York: Russell and Russell, Inc., 1934), 443-453, 201-205, and 611-674. There is also an excellent overview in Henry F. Salerno, *Scenarios of the commedia dell'arte: Flaminio Scala's Il teatro della favole rappresentative* (New York: New York University Press, 1967) 408-411. Louise George Clubb makes a persuasive case for Shakespeare borrowing not only plots but also techniques from *commedia erudita*, which used the three unities to hold together "imbroglio plots." See Clubb, "Italian stories on the stage," in *The Cambridge Companion to Shakespearean Comedy*, ed. Alexander Leggatt (Cambridge: Cambridge University Press, 2002), 34-38.

p. 40, par. 3, "a most dreadful tempest," from William Strachey, "The Voyages to Virginia, 1609-10," Virtual Jamestown, Virginia Center for Digital History, University of Virginia, p.1. http://virtualjamestown.org

p. 40, par. 4, William Strachey's letter and ""A True Declaration of the Estate of the Colonie in Virginia" (The Council of Virginia, 1610)" can be found at http://virtualjamestown.org. Excerpts from the relevant documents are also printed as appendices in Vaughan and Vaughan, Introduction to *The Tempest* (Arden[3]) and Stephen Orgel, Introduction to *The Tempest, by William Shakespeare*, (Oxford: Oxford UP, 1987). These editions, plus Frank Kermode, Introduction to *The Tempest, by William Shakespeare*, Arden Shakespeare, 2nd series (London: Methuen and Co., Ltd., 1954), have good overviews of the historical events. For more detail, see D.G. James, *The Dream of Prospero* (Oxford: Oxford University Press, 1967), 72-106.

p. 42, par. 1, Recent criticism has noted that Shakespeare may also have drawn on negative elements in the Jamestown and Bermuda documents, which cite "a tempest of dissension" and the "ooze" and "unwholesome vapor" of the swamps (see Virtual Jamestown, Virginia Center for Digital History, University of Virginia, 14-15. At http://etext.lib.virginia.edu/etcbin/jamestown-browse?id=J1059 or through the portal at http://virtualjamestown.org). The dissention is stressed in Stephen J. Greenblatt, "Martial law in the land of Cockaigne," in *Shakespearean Negotiations* (Berkeley: University of California Press, 1988), 94-163.

p. 42, par. 2, Gerald Graff and James Phelan, eds., *William Shakespeare, The Tempest: A case study in critical controversy* (Boston: Bedford/St. Martins, 2000) contains a good discussion of the critical debates, written for students, as well as several kinds of critical essays. The best criticism is both historically and critically informed. See, for example, John Gillies, "Shakespeare's Virginian Masque," in *The Tempest: Sources and Contexts, Criticism, Rewritings, and Appropriations*, ed. Peter Hulme and William H. Sherman (New York: W. W. Norton, 2004).

p. 42, par. 3, The dates for the romances and for the revisions of *King Lear* are conjectural. I've followed the *Oxford Companion to Shakespeare*, ed. Michael Dobson (Oxford: Oxford University Press, 2001), 533 and 244.

p. 42, par. 4, Edward Dowden stressed "the power of repentance" and "victory of love" (in Oxford Companion, 113-114, 395). See also Michael O'Connell, "The experiment of romance," in *The Cambridge Companion to Shakespearean Comedy*, ed. Alexander Leggatt (Cambridge: Cambridge University Press, 2002), 215. Frank Kermode finds in the romances "the mercy of a providence which gives new life when the old is scarred by sin or lost in folly," Kermode, Introduction to *The Tempest* (Arden²), lxi.

p. 54, par. 3, One aspiration of the Neoplatonist mage was to "walk to the skie" (Kermode, Introduction to *The Tempest* (Arden²), xli.

p. 76, par. 2, For the Medea speech in Arthur Golding's 1567 translation of Ovid's *Metamorphoses* (Bk. 7, 263-89) see http://www.elizabethanauthors. com/ovid07.htm

p. 78, par. 2, Stephen Orgel, Introduction to *The Tempest*, (Oxford: Oxford University Press, 1987), 55-56 and 204n.

p. 92, par. 1, For the classic discussion of the theme of metamorphosis and these lines see Reuben A. Brower's 1951 essay, "The mirror of analogy: *The Tempest*," in *Shakespeare The Tempest. A Casebook*, ed. D.J. Palmer (London: Macmillan and Co., 1969), 153-175.

p. 96, par. 2, On the use of the music of language to signal both harmony as resistance, see Jacquelyn Fox-Good, "Other voices: the sweet, dangerous air(s) of Shakespeare's Tempest," *Shakespeare Studies* 24 (1996), 241-75.

p. 97, par. 4, On Shakespeare's use of figures of interruption (parenthesis, hyperbaton, anastrophe) see Sister Miriam Joseph, *Shakespeare's Use of the Arts of Language* (Philadelphia: Paul Dry Books, 2005 [originally 1947]). 54-57. Sister Miriam says anastrophe (disruption of word order) "might almost be said to characterize the style of *The Tempest*," 54.

p. 98, par. 2, For a discussion of Shakespeare's uses of paronomasia and other figures of repetition, see Sister Miriam Joseph, 166 and 341. For Shakespeare's uses of epizuexis and diacope, see Sister Miriam, 86-88 and 307. Diacope is the repetition of a word with one or few between. Epizeuxis is repetition with no words between.

p. 99, par. 4, On Shakespeare's knowledge of Puttenham, see Sister Miriam Joseph, 44. The "slow return" is Puttenham's name for diacope (or according to other Rhetorics, epanalepsis), in "The Arte of English Poesie," 3.19. Here it is coupled with polyptoton (the repetition of words derived from the same root in different grammatical forms): *sleep*(noun)/ *sleep*(verb); *dreaming/dream*. Puttenham's "Art of English Poesie" is available online at the Electronic Text Center, University of Virginia Library, http://etext.lib.virginia/toc/modeng/publi/PutPoes.html. See also "Silva rhetoricae"(http://humanities.byu/rhetoric/silva.htm), a very useful website with cross-referenced information on rhetorical terminology.

p. 100, par. 2, "rich, irreducible concreteness," Stephen J. Greenblatt, "Learning to curse: aspects of linguistic colonialism in the sixteenth century," in *Learning to curse: essays in early modern culture* (New York: Routledge, 1990), 31.

p. 102, par. 1, "showcases...betrothal," Vaughan and Vaughan, Introduction to *The Tempest* (Arden[3]), 15.

p. 102, par. 2, "centerpiece...character groups," Mark Rose, *Shakespearean Design* (Cambridge, MA: Harvard University Press, 1972), 173.

p. 106, par. 4, On the parody of the masque, see Vaughan and Vaughan, Introduction to *The Tempest* (Arden[3]), 73.

A Shakespeare Glossary

The student should not try to memorize these, but only refer to them as needed. We can never stress enough that the best way to learn Shakespeare's language is simply to *hear* it—to hear it spoken well by good actors. After all, small children master every language on Earth through their ears, without studying dictionaries, and we should master Shakespeare, as much as possible, the same way.

addition — a name or title (knight, duke, duchess, king, etc.)
admire — to marvel
affect — to like or love; to be attracted to
an — if ("An I tell you that, I'll be hanged.")
approve — to prove or confirm
attend — to pay attention
belike — probably
beseech — to beg or request
betimes — soon; early
bondman — a slave
bootless — futile; useless; in vain
broil — a battle
charge — expense, responsibility; to command or accuse
clepe, clept — to name; named
common — of the common people; below the nobility
conceit — imagination
condition — social rank; quality
countenance — face; appearance; favor
cousin — a relative
cry you mercy — beg your pardon
curious — careful; attentive to detail
dear — expensive
discourse — to converse; conversation
discover — to reveal or uncover
dispatch — to speed or hurry; to send; to kill
doubt — to suspect

entreat — to beg or appeal

envy — to hate or resent; hatred; resentment

ere — before

ever, e'er — always

eyne — eyes

fain — gladly

fare — to eat; to prosper

favor — face, privilege

fellow — a peer or equal

filial — of a child toward his or her parent

fine — an end; "in fine" = in sum

fond — foolish

fool — a darling

genius — a good or evil spirit

gentle — well-bred; not common

gentleman — one whose labor was done by servants (Note: to call someone a *gentleman* was not a mere compliment on his manners; it meant that he was above the common people.)

gentles — people of quality

get — to beget (a child)

go to — "go on"; "come off it"

go we — let us go

haply — perhaps

happily — by chance; fortunately

hard by — nearby

heavy — sad or serious

husbandry — thrift; economy

instant — immediate

kind — one's nature; species

knave — a villain; a poor man

lady — a woman of high social rank (Note: *lady* was not a synonym for *woman* or *polite woman*; it was not a compliment, but, like *gentleman*, simply a word referring to one's actual legal status in society.)

leave — permission; "take my leave" = depart (with permission)

lief, lieve — "I had as lief" = I would just as soon; I would rather

like — to please; "it likes me not" = it is disagreeable to me livery — the uniform of a nobleman's servants; emblem

mark — notice; pay attention

morrow — morning

needs — necessarily

nice — too fussy or fastidious

owe — to own

passing — very

peculiar — individual; exclusive

privy — private; secret

proper — handsome; one's very own ("his proper son")

protest — to insist or declare

quite — completely

require — request

several — different; various

severally — separately

sirrah — a term used to address social inferiors

sooth — truth

state — condition; social rank

still — always; persistently

success — result(s)

surfeit — fullness

touching — concerning; about; as for

translate — to transform

unfold — to disclose

villain — a low or evil person; originally, a peasant

voice — a vote; consent; approval

vouchsafe — to confide or grant

vulgar — common

want — to lack

weeds — clothing

what ho — "hello, there!"

wherefore — why

wit — intelligence; sanity

withal — moreover; nevertheless

without — outside

would — wish

Suggested Essay Topics

1. How is reconciliation achieved in the play? Who is included in the reconciliation? Who is left out? Does it matter that everyone is not included? Why do you think Shakespeare ended the play this way?

2. Compare and contrast the stories of Prospero and Sycorax. How are they alike? How are they different? Why do you think Shakespeare made their stories so similar? What matters more, the similarities or the differences?

3. Miranda says, "I have suffered with those that I saw suffer," which defines "the very virtue of compassion." How does compassion become an issue in the resolution of the play? How does it figure in the Epilogue?

4. Prospero prides himself on being Miranda's teacher, and he is frustrated by his failures with Caliban. Does Caliban learn in the play? How does Caliban learn? Does Prospero learn? (You might want to consider Ariel as teacher at the beginning of Act V.) What does the play have to say about education?

5. Is the Epilogue a necessary part of the play, or is the play complete without it? How is the play different with and without the Epilogue? Why is it there?

6. Prospero stages four major spectacles in the play: the tempest (I.1), the banquet with the Harpy (III.3), the wedding masque (IV.1), and his "discovery" of Ferdinand and Miranda playing chess (V.1). How are these performances different from one another? What does their progression tell us about Prospero's development over the course of the play?

Testing Your Memory

1. Why does Prospero take off his magic robes before he tells Miranda the story of his life? a) He doesn't want her to know that he's a magician; b) He's talking to her as a father, not as a magician; c) He might accidentally perform a spell while he's talking to her; d) He's afraid the robes will frighten her.

2. Who is Antonio? a) Prospero's brother; b) the king of Naples; c) Sebastian's brother; d) Prospero's son.

3. How did Milan lose its independence? a) Milan lost a war with Naples; b) Prospero had no male heir, and so the dukedom went to Alonso, king of Naples; c) Antonio amassed huge debts that he could not repay, and the dukedom was forfeited; d) Antonio voluntarily surrendered the independence of Milan to Naples in exchange for aid in replacing Prospero as duke.

4. Who helps Prospero and the two-year-old Miranda survive when they are put out to sea? a) Alonso; b) Antonio; c) Gonzalo; d) Sebastian.

5. Where is the ship after Scene 1 of the play? a) hidden in a cove on the island; b) at sea; c) next to Prospero's cell but invisible; d) in Bermuda.

6. Who was Sycorax? a) Miranda's mother; b) Ariel's mother; c) Caliban's mother; d) Alonso's daughter, who was married in Tunis.

7. Who brushed the poisons off the swamps with a raven's feather? a) Ariel; b) Prospero; c) Caliban; d) Sycorax.

8. When did Caliban become Prospero's slave? a) when Prospero landed on the island; b) after Prospero freed Ariel from the pine; c) after Sycorax died; d) after Caliban tried to rape Miranda.

9. How does Ferdinand come to join Prospero and Miranda on the island? a) He swims from the ship and lands on the beach by Prospero's cell; b) He hears them talking and follows their voices; c) He follows Ariel's music, although he doesn't know where it's coming from; d) Ariel puts him in a trance and brings him.

10. Who mistakes Miranda for a goddess? a) Caliban; b) Antonio; c) Stephano; d) Ferdinand and Alonso.

11. Where was the ship traveling when it was struck by the tempest? a) from Tunis to Naples; b) from Algiers to Milan; c) from Naples to Carthage; d) from Milan to Tunis.

12. What is the four-legged monster Stephano discovers on the beach? a) a sea serpent; b) a Harpy: half woman and half bird of prey; c) Trinculo and Caliban under Caliban's cloak; d) a turtle with the face of a man.

13. Who carries logs in the play? a) Caliban and Ferdinand; b) Caliban and Trinculo; c) Trinculo and Stephano; d) Ferdinand and Stephano.

14. What does Caliban say Stephano must take away before he can kill Prospero? a) his books; b) his sword; c) his magic staff; d) his magic robes.

15. Who says the lines, "Be not afeard, the isle is full of noises, / Sounds, and sweet airs, that give delight and hurt not"? a) Ferdinand; b) Miranda; c) Caliban; d) Ariel.

16. What does Alonso do after the Harpy tells him it is his fault that his son has drowned? a) He refuses to believe it; b) He runs off to drown himself, too; c) He attacks the Harpy with his sword; d) He collapses in remorse and vows to change his life.

17. What do the goddesses Juno and Ceres do in the masque? a) They stop a drought that has brought famine to the world; b) They look for Venus and her son, Cupid; c) They bring a message to Iris from Jove; d) They bless the marriage of Ferdinand and Miranda.

18. How much time passes between the storm at the beginning of the play and the final scene? a) one day; b) three days; c) four hours; d) one week.

19. What does Antonio say in the last scene of the play? a) He begs Prospero's pardon; b) He thinks it would be possible to make money by displaying Caliban; c) He thinks Miranda is the goddess who has brought them all together; d) nothing.

20. What is Ariel's last task before being freed? a) to provide music while Prospero tells his story; b) to provide winds to blow Alonso's ship back to Naples; c) to provide clothing for Prospero and Miranda for the trip back; d) to sing Miranda to sleep.

Answer Key

Further Information

BOOKS

Hulme, Peter, and William H. Sherman, eds. *'The Tempest' and Its Travels.*
London: Reaktion Books, 2000.

——— . *The Tempest: Sources and Contexts, Criticism, Rewritings, and
Appropriations.* New York: W. W. Norton and Co., 2004.

Orgel, Stephen. Introduction to *The Tempest, by William Shakespeare*,
1–87. Oxford: Oxford University Press, 2008.

WEBSITES

Encyclopedia Britannica's Guide to Shakespeare.
http://shakespeare.eb.com

The Internet Shakespeare. Internet Shakespeare Editions, University of
Victoria. An excellent site with concise, peer-reviewed information on a
variety of topics.
http://internetshakespeare.uvic.ca

FILMS

The Tempest. Directed by John Gorrie. BBC Television Shakespeare (TV,
UK), 1980. U.S. Release (BBC/Time-Life) as part of "The Complete
Dramatic Works of William Shakespeare." Michael Hordern as
Prospero.

The Tempest. Directed by William Woodman. Quantum Leap, "The
Shakespeare Collection" (TV/video, USA), 1983. Efrem Zimbalist Jr. as
Prospero. (This also appears as "The Plays of William Shakespeare"
Vol. 9, DVD, 2001.)

ADAPTATIONS

Forbidden Planet. Directed by Fred M. Wilcox (USA), 1956.

Prospero's Books. Directed by Peter Greenaway (Netherlands, France, UK,
Italy), 1991.

Bibliography

Barker, Francis, and Peter Hulme. "Nymphs and Reapers Heavily Vanish: The Discursive Contexts of *The Tempest*." In *Alternative Shakespeares*, edited by John Drakakis, 191–205. London and New York: Methuen and Co., Ltd., 1985.

Bevington, David. "*The Tempest* and the Jacobean Court Masque." In *The Politics of the Stuart Court Masque*, edited by David Bevington and Peter Holbrook, 218–243. Cambridge: Cambridge University Press, 1998.

Bloom, Harold. *Shakespeare: The Invention of the Human*. New York: Penguin Group/Riverhead Books, 1998.

Bloom, Harold, ed. *William Shakespeare's The Tempest*. Modern Critical Interpretations. New York and Philadelphia: Chelsea House, 1988.

Brower, Reuben A. "The mirror of analogy: *The Tempest*." In *Shakespeare The Tempest. A Casebook,* edited by D. J. Palmer, 153–175. London: Macmillan and Co., 1969. Also reprinted in *William Shakespeare, The Tempest: A Case Study in Critical Controversy,* edited by Gerald Graff and James Phelan, 183–202. Boston: Bedford/St. Martins, 2000.

Brown, Paul. "'This thing of darkness I acknowledge mine': *The Tempest* and the Discourse of Colonialism." In *Political Shakespeare: New Essays in Cultural Materialism*, edited by Jonathan Dollimore and Alan Sinfield, 48–69. Ithaca: Cornell University Press, 1985.

Clubb, Louise George. "Italian Stories on the Stage." In *The Cambridge Companion to Shakespearean Comedy*, edited by Alexander Leggatt, 32–46. Cambridge: Cambridge University Press, 2002.

Fox-Good, Jacquelyn. "Other Voices: The Sweet, Dangerous Air(s) of Shakespeare's *Tempest*." Shakespeare Studies 24 (1996), 241–75, http://search.ebscohost.com/login.aspx?direct=true&db=aph&AN=9702184631&site=ehost-live" (accessed 7/4/2008).

Fuchs, Barbara. "Conquering Islands: Contextualizing *The Tempest*." In *The Tempest: Sources and Contexts, Criticism, Rewritings, and Appropriations,* edited by Peter Hulme and William H. Sherman, 265–285. New York: W. W. Norton and Co., 2004.

Gillies, John. "Shakespeare's Virginian Masque." In *The Tempest: Sources and Contexts, Criticism, Rewritings, and Appropriations,* edited by Peter Hulme and William H. Sherman, 265–285. New York: W. W. Norton and Co., 2004.

Greenblatt, Stephen J. "Learning to Curse: Aspects of Linguistic Colonialism in the Sixteenth Century." In *Learning to Curse: Essays in Early Modern Culture*, 16–39. New York: Routledge, 1990.

——— . "Martial Law in the Land of Cockaigne." In *Shakespearean Negotiations*, 94–163. Berkeley: University of California Press, 1988.

James, D. G. *The Dream of Prospero.* Oxford: Oxford University Press, 1967.

Lea, K. M. Italian Popular Comedy. *A Study in the Commedia dell'arte, 1560–1620, with Special Reference to the English Stage.* New York: Russell and Russell, Inc., 1934.

Lindley, David. "Music, Masque, and Meaning in *The Tempest.*" In *The Tempest: Sources and Contexts, Criticism, Rewritings, and Appropriations,* edited by Peter Hulme and William H. Sherman, 265–285. New York: W. W. Norton and Co., 2004.

Marcus, Leah. "The Blue-Eyed Witch." In *The Tempest: Sources and Contexts, Criticism, Rewritings, and Appropriations,* edited by Peter Hulme and William H. Sherman, 265–285. New York: W. W. Norton and Co., 2004.

Miriam Joseph, Sister. *Shakespeare's Use of the Arts of Language.* Philadelphia: Paul Dry Books, Inc., 2005 [Originally 1947].

Mowat, Barbara. "'Knowing I loved my books': Reading The Tempest Intertextually." In *'The Tempest' and Its Travels,* edited by Peter Hulme and William H. Sherman, 27–36. London: Reaktion Books, 2000.

———. "Prospero, Agrippa, and Hocus Pocus." In *The Tempest: Sources and Contexts, Criticism, Rewritings, and Appropriations,* edited by Peter Hulme and William H. Sherman, 265–285. New York: W. W. Norton and Co., 2004.

Nixon, Rob. "Caribbean and African Appropriations of *The Tempest.*" *Critical Inquiry* 13 (1987): 557–578.

O'Connell, Michael. "The Experiment of Romance." In *The Cambridge Companion to Shakespearean Comedy*, edited by Alexander Leggatt, 215–229. Cambridge: Cambridge University Press, 2002.

Palmer, D. J., ed. *Shakespeare: The Tempest. A Casebook.* London: Macmillan and Co., 1969.

Rose, Mark. *Shakespearean Design.* Cambridge, MA: Harvard University Press, 1972.

Salerno, Henry F., trans. *Scenarios of the Commedia dell'arte: Flaminio Scala's Il teatro della favole rappresentative.* New York: New York University Press, 1967.

Schneider Jr., Ben Ross. "'Are We Being Historical Yet?' Colonial interpretations of Shakespeare's *Tempest.*" *Shakespeare Studies* 23 (1995): 120–146.

Sokol, B. J. *A Brave New World of Knowledge: Shakespeare's "The Tempest" and Early Modern Epistemology.* Madison, NJ: Fairleigh Dickinson University Press, 2003.

Vaughan, Alden T. "Trinculo's Indian: American Natives in Shakespeare's England." In *'The Tempest' and Its Travels*, edited by Peter Hulme and William H. Sherman, 49–59. London: Reaktion Books, 2000.

Vaughan, Virginia Mason, and Alden T. Vaughan. *Shakespeare's Caliban: A Cultural History.* Cambridge: Cambridge University Press, 1991.

Zabus, Chantal. *Tempests after Shakespeare.* New York: Palgrave, 2002.

Index

Page numbers in **boldface** are illustrations.

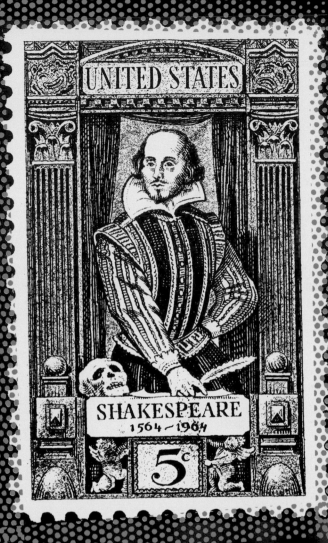

UNITED STATES

SHAKESPEARE
1564 – 1964

5ᶜ

About the Author

Susan H. Krueger received her PhD in comparative literature from Yale University in 1984. In the course of twenty-two years of college teaching at Williams College and Eugene Lang College at the New School, she taught *The Tempest* in courses on Shakespeare, Faust, literary theory, and T. S. Eliot's *The Waste Land*. She joined New York City Teaching Fellows in 2004, and currently teaches science and special education at a public school in the South Bronx.